A LOVE LETTER TO BUSINESS WRITING

Secrets of a Successful Freelancer

A LOVE LETTER TO BUSINESS WRITING

Secrets of a Successful Freelancer

HERMIONE ST. LEGER

MARVELLOUS BOOKS

Published by

MARVELLOUS BOOKS

12 St Peter's Place BN7 1YP
info@marvellousbooks.com
www.marvellousbooks.com
First Edition 2017

ISBN: 978-1-909900-08-0

Dedicated to Satyananda*

Contents

PART II: THE WORK

PART I: THE APPROACH

1   Becoming a freelance writer

Writing for the sheer joy of it

In the 1970s, *The Daily Gibber* was a household name...well, in one household, anyway. It was the brainchild of a young girl who liked nothing better than to interview unwitting (and sometimes unwilling) members of her family and publish the results. I would have liked to reproduce at least one article here, but they are all unprintable – too many political spoofs and family jokes!

But it didn't end there. There were stories, playlets and random musings galore – all written purely for the sake of entertainment. No story was ever finished and the content was never important – it was the sheer joy of writing that mattered.

This slowed down in my mid-teens as school work took over and maybe some self-consciousness, too. But the writing didn't stop, it was just expressed in other ways – mainly essays, particularly in History which I loved.

Indeed, another element crept in. I had a very wise teacher who told me that a good History essay did not simply present the facts; it should be a concise, well-argued exposition. To this end, no sentence must be wasted – or redundant.

Then I realised that I had another love: to argue a case – like a barrister in court – clearly, succinctly, persuasively. I didn't even mind what the case was particularly, it was the flow and clarity of argument that mattered.

In one exam, for example, I realised that I only had enough facts at my disposal to write the essay from one (unusual and slightly dubious) angle; and so I did, as persuasively as I could – and amazingly it worked! In fact, I was applauded for my original thinking (and by a History professor to boot).

It taught me that writing persuasively was not only enjoyable, it can be as important – sometimes even more so – than the facts themselves. Yet my love for the subject was genuine and there was never any doubt it was what I was going to study at university.

The peace of deep contemplation

It was here that a third element then revealed itself: the peace to be found in burying myself away and contemplating the work deeply. This could be in my college library, the Radcliffe Camera or my favourite – Duke Humfrey's Library at the Bodleian, Oxford.

Built in the fifteenth century, this was so peaceful and atmospheric it was like sitting in a medieval castle (which is why it also became Hogwarts library in the *Harry Potter* films). Unfortunately, you are only supposed to use it if you are actually studying its manuscripts and I was eventually rumbled and asked to leave! But I have never lost that love of studying quietly on my own.

So, with a good degree in my pocket, from a good university, the world was my oyster...wasn't it? It certainly didn't feel that way. Indeed, I found leaving all my friends so unsettling I decided I had to do something drastic – in this case, become an au pair in the South of France!

It was a great experience in many ways, but also a very lonely one, my employers requiring me to stay in every night while they ran their restaurant in St Tropez. So after six weeks, I made my excuses and left: first for Italy (where a friend lived), then Germany (where my sister lived). Two months later, I was in no hurry to come home, but an operation to remove my wisdom teeth soon put paid to that!

It was the beginning of a very difficult decade in which I had a succession of jobs, but none that felt truly right or comfortable. Always conscientious, I worked terribly hard, but fear was never far away; and fear, I came to realise, was a terrible 'blocker'.

Eventually, I ended up in sales promotion, where I at least enjoyed writing business proposals (it was only later I realised how much!).

But the first agency let me go and the second was a deeply unhappy experience: for six weeks I toiled desperately to make it work, but it was clear there would be no happy ending. Yes, I could move to another agency, but what was the point when I didn't actually enjoy the work itself?

I was 28 years old. What a mess...or so I thought.

It's never too late to change direction

Many years later, 28 years old now seems very young indeed. But age is relative and when life is not going the way you want it to, 28 doesn't feel young at all. On the contrary, you feel like a very 'old' young person. It's the same for every decade!

So it was a time of crisis; and as with so many crises, help came at the eleventh hour. The revelation came one night while I was driving across London, having dropped a friend off home. Maybe it came because I was focused on the driving, instead of thinking, thinking, thinking...

But when it came, it was clear and indisputable – I should be a freelance copywriter! It made perfect sense: I had always loved writing, I knew I was good at it and I knew precisely how the industry worked. In fact, I was never more sure of anything in my life. I couldn't wait to get started.

As for those who doubted the wisdom of this move – well, it made no difference whatsoever. This absolute conviction was needed in the months ahead as one does not become a copywriter overnight. You have to find the clients first!

But in case you conclude that all the preceding years were therefore wasted, let me assure you otherwise:

- Whilst the ability to write well is clearly requisite, writing for business also requires an acute commercial awareness that is grounded in reality – you never lose sight of the ultimate objective.

- Working in an agency environment instils in you an attitude of service and flexibility – especially important if you are freelance.

- Lastly, but importantly, the sense of gratitude at finally finding my 'métier' has never left me. It is important not only because gratitude is synonymous with joy – which in turn is reflected in your work – it also sustains you when the work is difficult or challenging.

Sometimes you need to do the 'wrong' job in order to appreciate the 'right' job when it finally materialises!

In fact, everything went full circle in the end...I later went back to the agency that had let me go to work as a freelance writer; and wrote conference speeches for an Account Director from the second agency when they moved client-side. This was very helpful in reconciling me to the difficulties of those early years.

If you really love writing, you'll find a way...

In hindsight, I realise that my love of writing manifested in almost every job – whether it was part of the job description or not. For example, when I worked for a consumer electronics firm as a humble Publicity Executive, they needed a new brochure for their state-of-the-art TVs. They commissioned a freelance writer but weren't happy with the result, so I eagerly volunteered.

In sales promotion, when writing a business proposal, I fully embraced the practice of cranking up the drama before finally revealing the idea. Even minutes to client meetings were treated with reverence (they had to be clear and succinct!).

It just never occurred to me that I could make a living out of it...

The darkest hour is before the dawn

So, I was now officially a freelance copywriter – it said so on my business card! Mindful that I needed to earn money while I tried to get work, I initially 'temped' as a secretary. But even continuous employment wasn't enough to stop me falling into debt: it was a time of deep recession and with a mortgage and interest rates as high as 15%, I was losing every month.

I knew I couldn't continue like this indefinitely, but surely a breakthrough would come soon? I was doing everything I could to make it happen: I stayed behind after work writing new-business letters to sales promotion/marketing agencies and chasing up those I had already sent. (Remember, this was before email and mobile phones became commonplace – I had to use public phone boxes!) I was very lucky that the two companies I temped for allowed me to use all their facilities – computer, copier, printer.

Interviews were not always a breeze, either: one man commented that my new-business letter was very good and did I write it? (!) Another made sleazy comments that put me right off working for him.

I made mistakes, too. Obviously, I had a very thin portfolio as I wasn't yet a working copywriter. Yes, I had some material from my time in sales promotion (and the TV brochure), but it was nowhere near enough. So I supplemented it with some leaflets I hadn't written, but on whose account I had worked. There was only one problem: they were very badly written! Imagine my horror when an interviewer drew one of these out of my portfolio, read it, then asked whether I had written it. I couldn't bear for him to think I had, so admitted the truth!

Mistakes aren't always what they seem

I have to be honest: I have a very different view of 'mistakes' now from when I was younger, when I imagined that if I made one, the consequences could never be rectified.

It's not true!

I now feel that as long as you try your best, it's okay to make mistakes sometimes; in fact, it's natural. When I look back, I also realise that so-called mistakes never resulted in any lasting damage, yet taught me valuable lessons from which I later benefited (usually when it *really* mattered).

I would go further: 'mistakes' (such as fluffing an interview or relationship) have actually been blessings, as I realised later that I was saved from a situation that would not have been good or helpful – or something much better came along. How, then, can you call them mistakes?

Back then, however, it would never have occurred to me to think in such a way...

Finally, after several months, I admitted to my nearest and dearest just how worried I was. They were sympathetic and tried to reassure me, but of course they couldn't influence the situation.

I felt very alone.

Having the courage of your convictions

But the very next week – at the eleventh hour again! – the breakthrough came. I was given a piece of work from a sales promotion agency. This led to more and more...until three months later, they offered me a full-time job!

Now, this was a very tricky situation: on the one hand, I didn't want to lose my one and only client; on the other, even after this short time, I realised how much I enjoyed the freedom of being freelance. It was a dilemma, but not one I contemplated for long.

I followed my heart and turned down the job. That December was very uncertain, with no money coming in and Christmas presents to buy, but I held my nerve and wrote new-business letters instead. (I later learnt that December is invariably a damp squib work-wise!) But come the New Year, the letters paid off and two brand new clients materialised.

Incidentally, knowing when to leave my temp job was also tricky. As I took more and more time off to do copywriting work, the senior secretary warned me that if I wasn't careful, I would be "shown my cards" (i.e. fired). But while this was meant to sound alarming, I thought: "But I don't *want* to be a temporary secretary – I want to be a copywriter!"

I certainly wasn't going to turn down any copywriting work that came my way, so after six months temping I finally flew the nest...

I was on my own now!

How creative *is* business writing?

Occasionally people have said to me, "Wouldn't you like to write creatively?" and my instinct is to feel very frustrated! Writing for business could not *be* more creative: you have a totally blank canvas on which to paint any picture, any way you like.

Yes, you always have an objective, but you could say that about any writing – even if the objective is simply to make people laugh or spin a good story. The joy is in the writing not the content – and this is transmitted inexorably to the reader. The challenge: to transform *any* message on *any* subject into a clear, compelling and enjoyable read.

And you don't get more creative than that...

N.B. In the interests of readability, I have contracted some words (e.g. "didn't" instead of "did not") and started some sentences with "And" or "But". This may be perfectly okay for consumer-driven communications (and speeches), but is not usually appropriate for more formal business materials.

2   The joy of being freelance

The freedom of working from home

At first it felt very strange to work on my own at home after years of working with others. I would pace up and down, nibbling biscuits and drinking tea in a frantic attempt to get inspiration!

But the feeling didn't last...in fact, I found it relaxing being away from all the noise and politics of the workplace, allowing me to focus totally on the job in hand; and every morning I heard my neighbour rush out to work, I was so grateful it wasn't me. As for those who say that they would get distracted too easily working from home, let me tell you – the need to earn money soon sorts that out!

Working from home also allows you to work odd hours: late into the night or very early in the morning. Sometimes this is essential, either to meet a tight deadline or to take advantage of the absolute quiet. I have even had to work *through* the night on several occasions and while this is not sustainable and always a last resort, I have to say: the peace is magical. There is usually the opportunity to rest (even for just a little while!) when it's all over.

Whilst you seldom have the luxury of waiting for creativity to arise, having a break at a time of your choosing can also be critical to clear your head. There is no virtue in staring at a screen if there's no clarity. But that doesn't mean that time is wasted; after all, at home you can do whatever you want – chores, paperwork, even some badly needed exercise! (It's not healthy to sit for hours without a break.)

You must be able to focus!

Of course, there are also downsides to working from home, the biggest being that it can be hard to switch off. For this reason, I did try renting office space for several months in an agency that was also a client.

Initially, it made a nice change. But it soon turned out to be more trouble than it was worth: not only did it take 45 minutes to get there (too long when you have an urgent job to do), there was no Internet connection for me either (this was long before Wi-Fi!).

Most damaging of all, however, were the constant noise and interruptions: when I work, I focus totally on what I'm doing and don't want to break off much to chat. But that didn't stop other people...

So I ended the experiment and came to appreciate what I actually had: a quiet place to work where I could totally focus, any time I needed to. Whether you work at home or in a rented office, alone or with others – *that's* what really matters.

Being at peace with the unknown

One of the key characteristics of being freelance is, of course, the insecurity. At the beginning this was acute as I had no savings, no clients and no long-term security. But when you are 100% sure that you want to do something, and believe totally that you can do it, this gives you courage and drive. This acute stage also doesn't last forever because over time you gradually build up experience, clients – and savings.

But the insecurity forced me to look at life in a different way: when you are freelance you can't possibly worry about the next 20 years, the next 10 years, or even the next year – it's just not realistic. You would spend your entire life worrying! When taken to its logical conclusion, you realise that life is not lived year by year, month by month, or even week by week – it's moment by moment!

This realisation had an interesting effect on me, which has never left: the knowledge that everything can change in a moment. So even though, on one level, weeks and months can appear to pass in a flash, these are made up of millions of moments when so much can be done – and anything can happen.

In practical terms, it meant that if I didn't have any work, I could do a great deal to change that in just one day (write new-business letters etc.); and if I didn't have any work for the first three weeks in any month, a big project could suddenly come along that changed everything.

In short, I had no choice but to expect the unexpected – and be at peace with it.

Confidence is reassuring – for you *and* your client

So, you are in the final week of the month, nothing has come in and you are starting to panic a bit. It's natural.

So when a client rings up and asks whether you are free, what do you say? "Absolutely – I haven't had any work for ages!" Of course not. You handle yourself with dignity, as always. You can still be enthusiastic – indeed, you should be – but it is the enthusiasm of someone who is confident and in constant work, not relieved that they have finally got a job.

Your reply? "Yes, actually it's perfect timing – I've *just* finished a job!" Such confidence is reassuring for your client – and makes you feel better, too.

In order to give my mind some semblance of control, however, I worked out how much I needed to earn every month to break even and at the beginning of every month the stopwatch would start again... In fact, I would assume that I had *already* lost this amount to avoid the worry of time slipping by without any work. So when it did come in, it was a bonus!

All mind games, but if it helps to keep you calm and focused, no problem. Indeed, the reality was that work *did* come in month after month, year after year. It wasn't consistent of course – some months there was nothing, others were extremely busy – and I never knew which direction it was going to come from.

But if I undertook one piece of work for a client, they usually gave me more and more, so there was a thread of continuity that gradually grew stronger and stronger, and client relationships that lasted years. One even turned into a de facto permanent job, though I can only say that in hindsight as I never actually knew what was going to happen from one month to the next...

Don't waste precious 'quiet time' worrying

In the early years, it's quite understandable to fear a 'quiet time', particularly when you don't have a lot of savings. It may well be that this is the perfect time to seek new business and if the urge is there, you must absolutely follow it.

But after some years, I realised that it wasn't quite as simple as that. Sometimes, after a period of intense activity, the quiet time was there for a reason: to enable me to rest and the worst thing I could do was ruin it by worrying.

For example, there was one nine-month period when I had very little work, just enough to get by. But the very thought of seeking new business felt wrong. So I followed my intuition and took it easy, knowing that any day I could change my mind and go for it.

Then, out of the blue, I was given a project that was not only extensive in itself, it led to years' of continuous work, with very few breaks. I realised later that the quiet time had been essential to prepare for this. It also meant that I had the *capacity* to undertake all the new work which came my way (I did have other clients but nothing that interfered unduly – I just worked very hard!). But the same principle can also apply to short periods of rest.

You just need to be very subtle and listen to your intuition – not fear!

Learning to trust the flow of life

I also began to see a pattern emerging: given the uncertainty of the work, I obviously said yes to everything if I possibly could. But given that I worked for several clients at any time, projects often threatened to overlap if one went on longer than expected, or a deadline changed. At the same time, deadlines were usually tight and non-negotiable.

But time and again I was saved by events: projects would suddenly be put back or cancelled, giving me the breathing space I needed to fulfil all the work that came my way. Amazingly, I never had to let anyone down. This happened so many times that I started to trust that maybe life wasn't so chaotic after all...

It wasn't obvious at first, but after years of being freelance, I couldn't deny it: seeing the flow of work come and go – just at the right time, in just the right way – imbued in me a deep conviction that everything works out for the best in the end.

I even noticed this synchronicity when working for the *same* organisation for many years. The subject was very complex and fast-moving, but every piece of work – even if on a different topic, working for different people – seemed to link to the previous one, allowing me to run with it from the very start.

There is a natural career path

It seems that everything has a cycle: even business relationships that have lasted years must end eventually, either because the work has finished or the client has moved jobs, or even retired. Some jobs, on the other hand, never lead to anything much, but are very welcome at the time.

You never know what will happen: one company made me go through hoops in order to secure a place on their 'preferred supplier' list, even though I had been working for them for several years (it wasn't just me, it was a national initiative). I succeeded – then never heard from them again! But it didn't matter as another client then came along...

There has to be a cycle to some degree – either through choice or circumstance – otherwise there would be no 'progression'. After 20 years, you would still be writing about, for example, food or beauty products (neither of which I would like to do now!).

When you are freelance, there is no official career path and yet it seems to happen anyway as your experience and responsibilities grow. It seems a natural outcome when you are dedicated and always willing to help and take the initiative.

Taking the initiative is a way of life

Once you have come to terms with the insecurity, being freelance therefore gives you confidence: you are totally responsible for yourself and your work. You don't lean on anyone and you don't feel the victim of anyone. You are accountable to your clients, yes, but that's not a problem – you accept and embrace that. But you are not accountable to anyone else – there is no middle man! – and that gives you the confidence to use your initiative and give your best.

After all, clients are not paying you to deliver good work. They are paying you to deliver excellent work – every time. You could call this pressure, but in fact it keeps you motivated, while the unpredictability keeps it exciting.

Indeed, while the lack of an official job description can sometimes be frustrating, it also means that the sky is the limit as far as your input is concerned. While you are theoretically being employed to write, you invariably get involved in other areas such as marketing, strategy and project management – especially if you work directly for the company. But if this is supposed to happen, it will happen naturally: you should always respond to need as opposed to forcing the issue (see **Chapter 10: "Supporting your client"**).

Don't wait to be asked – just do it!

One day, out of the blue, I was asked to write a 40-page report for a stakeholder forum on behalf of my client. Of course I said yes, but the task could not have been more daunting: it was on a subject I knew nothing about and I had 10 days to complete it! But I was determined and worked every hour I could until the job got done. It was very stressful, but it worked: the first draft was well received.

However, being a stakeholder forum, this was then distributed not only to its members and their companies, but policymakers and even external consultants; and, naturally, everyone had a comment to make – sometimes totally contradictory! Initially, I was taken aback as I wasn't used to so much feedback; most of what I wrote basically got published verbatim.

As always, I had no formal brief or job description, but it came naturally to try and resolve issues myself rather than bothering my (very busy) client. Indeed, as a neutral figure, I was often best placed to do so. As Editor, I also had a very clear idea of what worked and what didn't. Finally, I didn't take any short cuts: I was prepared to discuss the issue for as long as it took in order to reach an amicable conclusion.

The moral of the story? As long as your initiative comes from a genuine desire to help, it will always be appreciated – and welcomed.

Money is more flexible than you think

For the first few years, I often worked for agencies – after all, they had the work and it was an easy way to access it. This also enabled me to build up a portfolio covering a wide range of sectors – finance, technology, IT, automotive, travel, property, health and beauty, food and drink – you name it, I wrote about it!

Then something happened to change my view: I started working for a well-known bank via a marketing agency. This went very well for a few years...until the agency stopped paying me. It wasn't obvious at first – agencies seldom pay within 30 days and sometimes use delaying tactics; they may even be waiting to be paid by the company themselves. I did not see any immediate cause for concern and in any case was fully occupied doing other work.

Well, you can guess the outcome...the agency never did pay me and in fact went bust, costing me a significant amount of money. Now it so happened that during the same period, I invested £10,000 in (what turned out to be) a very risky investment; so risky, I lost the lot when someone higher up in the chain went off with the money.

This was a very difficult time as although I had accumulated some savings by this time, it still represented a huge chunk – not to mention hours of hard work! Yet work continued to come in which helped sustain a feeling of normality.

In fact, I learnt some very interesting lessons, as it turned out that it was far from the disaster it first appeared to be:

- When I spoke to my accountant, I learnt that I actually had £9,000 more than I realised (in those days I had to pay tax in advance).

- As the money came from my savings, my day-to-day life was unaffected. Indeed, it is now clear that over a lifetime, this loss will make no difference whatsoever.

- Rather than dwell on the loss, I consciously let it go – only to receive nearly £4,000 back from the risky investment a few years later, just before I went on holiday to New Zealand (it paid for the holiday!). In fact, I had let it go so completely that it actually felt like a bonus, not money I had lost and regained!

- There was even a happy ending on the work front: the bank now employed me directly, instead of via the agency, beginning a long and fruitful relationship.

- It wasn't even the end of the agency: they contacted me a few years later – reformed and renamed – and offered me more work! I agreed, but on one condition: I would invoice their client directly this time.

Agency or direct client?

This wasn't the only time an agency went bust on me, though on that occasion I managed to get paid before it actually happened. However, these experiences were enough to convince me that I should work directly for companies instead.

With my agency background, I was used to dealing with clients, so it seemed like a natural progression. Of course I still worked for agencies if they asked me, but I no longer approached them myself.

Going direct proved a blessing in every way – and not just financially. When you work directly for the company you get far more involved, on every level, and it is here that your input and initiative really start to bear fruit...

This wasn't the only lesson I learnt about money. I began to notice that whenever I had a large, unexpected outlay – such as a new roof or dental work – more work always came in. In the early days, this was a lifesaver. While it was frustrating to see the extra money disappear so quickly, I also appreciated that it was a gift – *I always had enough for what I needed at the time.*

But the truth is that I have always seen *every* job as a gift. How can you not when you never know what's going to happen or where the work's going to come from?

Your intuition knows more than you do!

A self-employed person finds it notoriously difficult to take a holiday – you are scared of missing any work and there's no holiday pay! But here again, your intuition can come to the rescue...

For example, when a gap appeared in my work schedule, it seemed the perfect opportunity to take off. I started the process of booking the holiday and got all the way to the end, until the final 'BOOK' button. But I couldn't click it! I hesitated and hesitated, until in the end I had no choice but to abort mission.

I found it very distressing – what was wrong with me? Why was I prevaricating? Well, I found out the following morning...

I received a phone call asking if I could write a speech for a senior executive in an organisation I already worked for – and could I start straightaway? Not only was this a good job in itself, but as the first piece of work I undertook for this particular executive, it led to years' of continuous work thereafter. Then I understood: it was my intuition that had warned me and I never viewed apparent indecision in the same way again.

There is a corollary to this: I once went on holiday for a month to Australia while working for the bank mentioned above. Now as the work was very regular, I knew they would have to employ someone else in my absence, which made me a bit nervous. What if they preferred them to me?

However, not only were my fears unrealised, my client actually became even more appreciative: apparently, my stand-in had done a terrible job and they were relieved when I came back so I could redo it!

How to surf the waves of self-employment

1. Be good at what you do
2. Enjoy taking the initiative
3. Trust your intuition
4. Be personable and diplomatic
5. CARE!

3   Winning the business

First impressions count

It may sound obvious, but some people don't realise the critical importance of presentation. But when you first make contact with a potential client they know absolutely nothing about you, so have no choice but to make a judgement based on how you present yourself:

- An attractive and professional letterhead is a prerequisite – ideally, created by a professional graphic designer (I was lucky: a friend did mine).

- The same goes for your business card. It should be a 'solid', high quality card that shouts confidence and professionalism – not some cheap, flimsy thing that costs next to nothing.

- Ideally, you will also have a domain name, which looks more professional than an obviously personal email address (though admittedly I had one for years and it didn't do me any harm).

What's in a name?

You would think there would only be one term to describe someone who writes for business, but life is richer than that...you can be a copywriter, a business writer, a corporate writer – even a professional writer!

It's important to choose the right term, as that will define you. For example, I initially called myself a Copywriter ("Creative Copywriter"

---

in fact!) as I was working mainly for agencies and that was the recognised term. However, when I started writing speeches as well, I became a "Copywriter & Speechwriter" instead. But that didn't last either...

When I started working for European stakeholder fora, my responsibilities increased further to managing as well as writing reports, speeches and other communications. This meant negotiating with a broad range of members in order to maximise impact, reconcile business interests and find solutions that were attractive to all.

As "Copywriter" didn't do justice to this, I changed my title to "Corporate Writer" – and, so far, this has stood!

Your new-business letter is your first project

Potential clients don't need to look far to assess your writing skills – your new-business letter is enough! So take as long as you need to get this right; it is too important to rush and once you have nailed the template, it will serve you for a long time.

You need to come from the premise that no one will be interested in this unsolicited communication. That is not meant to be a confidence-zapping statement, but rather an incentive to make it as clear, succinct and persuasive as possible:

- One way to avoid a heavy (heart-sinking) block of text – but still make all your points – is to have an introductory sentence, followed by several bullets containing key messages. This breaks up the text and automatically makes the letter look brief and easy to digest.

- These bullets should state (briefly) what you have to offer and the key advantages of working with you. Don't be flowery or boastful about this; keep it precise and professional.

- A good freelance writer should be able to write about *any* subject: you become adept at assimilating information, sorting the 'wheat from the chaff' and extracting the key messages. Nevertheless, it's always reassuring for clients to know that you have already worked in their sector, so one bullet should focus on relevant experience/accounts if at all possible.

- Finish with a sign-off sentence offering to meet and show them your portfolio; in the meantime, you attach a few samples of work for their consideration. It is quality not quantity that matters, so two may be enough, otherwise you risk overwhelming the client with too much information.

New-business letters should obviously be followed up with a phone call, but give them a couple of days – the intention is to make it easy for them, not harass them!

Dressing the part

Presentation extends to what you wear, too, and the rule is very simple: dress how you wish to be perceived. So if you want to show that you are highly professional, you dress as if you were attending an important meeting, accompanied by a smart briefcase or similar. If you are aiming at agency work, there is obviously a much more relaxed dress code, but you can still look professional: sloppy dress says sloppy work.

In the early days, when I had no money to spare, I remember agonising over whether to buy a new handbag as the current one was quite battered. Then I realised that I needed to think in terms of years, not months. A battered handbag would give the wrong impression to potential clients; *not* buying a new one was therefore a false economy.

It doesn't matter if you only have one new-business outfit – just make sure it is a good one!

It must have been a nice briefcase

In my early twenties, before I became a freelance writer, a friend once remarked to me that I was obviously very professional. Puzzled, I asked why he said this when he had never worked with me. He thought for a moment then said: "Because you carry a briefcase."

That's the power of presentation!

Anything is possible – so go for what you want!

If you are very clear about what you want – and know you can do it – there is absolutely no reason why it should not happen (and if it doesn't, it's because it's not meant to). *You just need to go for it!*

For example, after several years, I realised that I particularly enjoyed writing speeches. After all, arguing a case was second nature to me and nothing offers greater freedom to do this than speechwriting. So without further ado, I wrote to the Chairman of a large, multinational company offering my services. He forwarded my letter to the head of their speechwriting panel...and guess what? They were looking for another speechwriter!

This not only led to numerous speeches across a variety of areas, but many other projects, spanning years; and all because of one new-business letter...

Feeling nervous?

Winning the business can be a nerve-wracking process if you want it very badly (which you usually do!). In this respect, it's no different from any job interview. So how do you stay cool under pressure? It's no good trying to persuade yourself that you are not bothered when you obviously are...

Just a couple of years after becoming freelance, I had to give a client presentation with my graphic designer friend on our ideas for a range of sales materials. I desperately wanted the job and asked a wise friend of mine if he had any advice on how I could control my nerves. He replied, "Listen. Listen so hard it hurts."

The rationale? When you focus your attention on something else – in this case, listening – fear automatically recedes because you are no longer feeding it. It's like a form of meditation. This doesn't just mean listening to others, it means listening to yourself as you speak, or if no one is talking, to the sounds in the room or outside.

I did as he suggested and it worked – and we got the job!

One project can set off a whole chain of events

Indeed, looking back over 20-odd years' of work, it is clear that very little happens in isolation: a single project has often led to a whole stream of work, often lasting years. One recommendation leads to another and another, until you can hardly remember where it all began.

The truth is, if this doesn't happen, then something is wrong. You shouldn't have to write new-business letters every month, except maybe in the early years. Your client should be so happy with your work that they have no hesitation in giving you more and this eventually creates some stability. There is then a ripple effect: the longer you work, the more you become established – and the greater the frequency and regularity of the work.

It all started with one client...

An Account Director in the very first agency I worked for moved to another agency in London. There, along with other accounts, I worked (remotely) for the German arm of an international technology company.

This company also ran a major operation in Barcelona and I was asked if I would like to work there for a few months, writing a presentation for an exciting new product range. I didn't speak any Spanish, but that didn't matter – the in-house language was English and the Marketing department was full of expats.

It was a very intense but rewarding experience; so good that when I returned home, I decided I wanted to repeat it straightaway! Perusing the company's European offices, I saw one based in Bergamo, Italy. "That sounds nice", I thought, and immediately made contact.

As luck would have it, there was indeed a project available and while I didn't live there this time, I did visit for a week and work remotely for three months. The whole process was then repeated again for another product area in France.

The moral of the story? You just need to ask!

Getting the work is not the end of the story, of course. It's just the beginning...

4   Doing the business

Just start and the 'knots' will gradually unravel

At first, any project can seem like a daunting task: there you are, with your laptop open...where on earth do you start?

The answer is simple – you just start! This is not as facile as it appears. The truth is that once you start, it is inevitable that confusion will slowly give way to clarity *one step at a time*. You just need to take that leap of faith. Everything else is delaying tactics.

At this early stage, it is crucial to really focus and not get distracted, otherwise you will never succeed in diving deep, the 'links' will not happen in your mind and you will continue to skate around on the surface. Once you are 'in it', however, the way then opens up and gradually everything becomes clearer and clearer. That's when you really start to enjoy the process as insights gather apace.

It's a bit like doing a jigsaw puzzle: in the beginning, it looks so difficult you feel like giving up before you have even started. Then once you are in the flow, one piece leads to another, then another...until you are almost watching your hands moving, instead of controlling them!

For this reason, you should never send work to a client before it is finished – however much they ask. This is because you know that the deeper you go into the work, the more likely it is that you will change your mind. By the end, you are an expert in your own project and may well disagree with the initial ideas you had as a beginner!

If your client wishes to see a suggested structure first, this is not unreasonable, but it should be given with the proviso that it may change once you have gone deeper into the work.

Clarity comes one step at a time

In fact, experience eventually teaches you that you can do the most difficult jobs, with the most difficult deadlines, on subjects of which you have absolutely no knowledge.

You don't panic in the way you used to because you no longer expect to have all the answers straightaway – it is never like that – it is always one step at a time. You have Eureka moments, yes, but it is impossible to know every word or message you will write in advance, just as it would be impossible to complete a 1,000-piece jigsaw in five minutes!

Nevertheless, in my mind's eye, I often imagine the finished product – not in any detail, but in an indefinable sense that it exists (successfully) in the future and is just waiting to be realised. It's a bit like a sculptor saying that the sculpture already exists within the wood or stone – their job is simply to reveal it. Such visualisation can be very helpful because it gives the sense that the work is absolutely doable and that you are simply working step by step towards its realisation.

It's always moment by moment

I have had exactly the same experience writing this book...every day I wonder what I will write and every day new ideas come. But I never know beforehand! I only know in that moment.

So many times I have thought, "What on earth shall I say next?" and the next day inspiration comes. Or at end of the day I feel tired and 'stuck' and the following morning, clarity comes again...

It is important to have this understanding as it takes away a lot of the pressure. Of course, experience eventually teaches you anyway, but why wait for experience? Enjoy that reassurance now!

Subtlety is the key

Writing will always reflect your personality and where you 'come from'. So if you have a calm, clear mind, your writing will naturally be clear and succinct. If, on the other hand, you rather like the sound of your own voice, your writing is likely to be long-winded and verbose. This may sound obvious, but it means that your inner state is very important – not just to the quality of the writing, but the efficiency with which it is executed.

In order to have clarity, you need to be very subtle – without ego or a desire for glory. If calmness is not felt naturally, meditation can help to settle a confused and agitated mind. It also gives you a feeling of space into which ideas can come without pressure. However, if the overriding desire is to do a good job for your client, you will naturally find a way that works for you.

As for me, my experience is that you hear (and see) the flow of words, noticing immediately if anything is out of place or jars – a bit like music!

Focus removes fear

While there is always a sweet feeling of relief when a job has finished successfully, *your focus is never on the end result, it is on the process.* Don't waste time and energy worrying about how your work will be received in the future. If your focus is on the here and now – moment by moment – the end result will take care of itself, naturally. (This also means not worrying about the next job before the present one is finished – it will simply scatter your attention to the detriment of both jobs!)

This does not mean that fear is the enemy. It is natural to be afraid sometimes – it shows how much the work means to you. It can also keep you alert and on your toes.

However, fear can also block creativity, but that is easily remedied and focus is the key. If your attention is 100% on the work, there is literally no space for fear so it will inevitably recede; and if you genuinely care about the work, you will focus naturally – in a relaxed way, without striving. Here again, meditation can help enormously to quieten your mind so you can do this. The ability to focus is like any muscle – the more you use it, the easier it gets!

You must also be in control of any distractions. If you get a lot of emails/texts/calls, be honest about your ability to concentrate if your phone is constantly pinging. Even if you don't respond, it's almost impossible to resist looking to see who it is – thus breaking your train of thought. So don't think twice about switching off facilities temporarily, or making your phone silent. Without the ability to concentrate, for a reasonable period of time, you will never dive deep enough to obtain clarity.

Keep your feet on the ground

With experience, you will naturally gain confidence in your judgement and work. But in the beginning you may be feeling your way...

One of my very first jobs was to write a leaflet for an agency promoting electronic goods. Mindful that my business card said that I was a "*Creative* Copywriter", I felt pressurised to come up with something that justified that epithet. So I wrote the text in rhyming couplets! It actually wasn't bad at all, but it wasn't what the client wanted and I had to rewrite it the 'normal' way.

It taught me four valuable lessons:

1. Clarity never comes from fear.

2. Creativity doesn't have to mean wacky – your idea still has to be professionally sound.

3. There is a big difference between putting your heart into something – and trying too hard (through fear).

4. If you have an idea that you believe in, but could be controversial – *tell your client first*. If they don't like it, you won't have wasted your time on something you won't get paid for; if they do like it – great, you have the green light!

You are capable of more than you think

It is important to recognise that while some jobs can be extremely challenging (e.g. the subject is new and very technical), these ultimately provide the greatest job satisfaction. Why? Because the more difficult the subject, the deeper the dive within. Only then do you realise a) how much you are actually capable of and b) that the answer always comes in the end...

When faced with a difficulty, the worst thing you can do is to panic and search desperately for a solution; inspiration doesn't visit a panicking mind. The *best* thing you can do is to contemplate the issue quietly and wait patiently for the Eureka moment to arrive...it always does.

If you are not in the right mood, simply switch your attention to something else and come back to it later, if you can. Sometimes letting a problem go is the only way to calm down your mind so that you have clarity when you look at it afresh.

After many weeks or months of intense work, you then enjoy the sweet relief of a happy ending!

Don't be afraid of the difficult jobs!

Years ago, I had to write a presentation on a range of computers which was extremely technical – and I knew nothing about computers then. Unfortunately, the agency rep who briefed me had no idea what it was all about either!

Since it wasn't in my nature to admit defeat, I cheerfully accepted the job and it was only on the train going home, with a mountain of paper on my lap, that I thought, "Oh God, have I bitten off more than I can chew here?"

Then, as time went on, I realised that I had two jobs: 1) to do the work and 2) to reassure my client. Every day I would tell him that everything was under control and every day I wondered if I was ever going to make it. With no one to turn to for advice, I spent hours searching the Internet for the meaning of technical terms and didn't stop until I found the answer. It was like scrambling around in the dark without a light.

But gradually, very gradually, it all became clearer and, amazingly, actually turned out well! Indeed, after the project ended, I met my client again and he said to me: "Every day, I thanked God you were there. I hadn't a clue what was going on and you were always so reassuring." And I thought: "If only you knew!"

I realised then that with time, patience and effort, I could understand and write about anything...

Details, details...

Even if you know that the layout will change at the design stage, it is essential that your client sees an immaculate draft from you first, otherwise how can they review it properly? Attention to detail is therefore critical and your client will rely on you to check everything: minor mistakes, even in draft text, do not breed confidence. This means undertaking a thorough proofread prior to submission.

For reports it gets even more complicated, with duplicate references and footnotes all requiring constant vigilance in the face of revisions. Just one revised sentence, on the other hand, can throw the entire pagination out! You therefore need to find the most succinct way to incorporate revisions – not just for its own sake, but in order to keep the structure/presentation intact.

If you also manage the design and print, the consequences are even more critical. For this reason, it's very helpful to employ a professional proofreader to check the finished artwork before going to print. Even though you will obviously check it yourself – as well as suggest any design revisions needed – a fresh pair of eyes is more likely to spot errors and you can relax knowing that everything is covered.

Be clear about money matters

Payment can be a tricky area as there is a big difference between being flexible – and a pushover. Your terms should be 30 days and while many companies will wait longer than that to pay you, you need to keep an eye on the situation. Don't be afraid to make a (polite) nuisance of yourself – some agencies will only pay on this basis!

Larger companies are generally reliable. However, if you are owed money, it is only reasonable to request payment before undertaking any new work – especially if you have a niggling feeling that all may not be well with your client's finances. If the alarm bells are really ringing, trust your instincts and walk away (once you have been paid!).

It goes without saying that you need to have an accountant, not only for the sake of your tax return, but so that you are clear about what you can and cannot claim on expenses. It is also important to be registered for VAT, even if your turnover doesn't reach the threshold when it becomes mandatory.

This is because:

- It looks more professional

- It allows you to claim VAT on a range of expenses

- The workload is minimal

- It makes no difference financially to your client (they can also claim it back).

I make no comment about rates and quotations as that is something you have to work out for yourself. However, the following principles may help:

1. *Believe in yourself and what you can deliver*: anyone can call themselves a copywriter/speechwriter/corporate writer etc., but the quality of the output – and the contribution of the writer – may not be the same.

2. *Be realistic* about how long it will take to do the project well, including:

    - Undertaking any additional research (if necessary)

    - Contemplating the subject matter deeply (especially where complex and/or sensitive) in order to determine the key messages

    - Refining the text (the draft you send your client will never be your first)

    - Incorporating any subsequent revisions (this will always be guesswork, but you need to allow some time).

3. *Always charge what you believe to be fair* – for you *and* your client. Being greedy is as harmful as underselling yourself. You don't need to discuss this principle with anyone, but if you genuinely want to be fair, the answer will come.

4. *Trust your intuition*: if you feel happy and motivated about the job, your fee is probably right; if you feel unhappy and/or a little exploited, you are probably being paid too little. (Your intuition will only be trustworthy if you are rock solid about Principle No. 3.)

Quoting for jobs is never easy – particularly in the early days – so don't beat yourself up if you find it difficult to work out; experience teaches you eventually. If you honestly feel that you have significantly underestimated the time, or revisions are far greater than you anticipated (through no fault of your own), then you can tactfully raise this with your client. But it has to be justified or they won't take kindly to this unexpected change in the budget; and the sooner you raise it the better – don't spring it on them *after* the job is all over!

There are no strict rules, however, so in the final analysis, follow your intuition. Sometimes it's better to cut your losses and simply learn from experience when quoting for the next job (either for the same or a different client).

Trust your own judgement

Everyone doubts themselves sometimes – it's natural. No one has the definitive answer to everything. Indeed, you could argue no such thing exists. If it did, there would only be one perfect version of, say, an exam essay, whereas clearly there are as many possibilities as there are students!

To put it another way, if you were to ask 100 people for their views on something, you would receive 100 different responses – all very, or at the very least, slightly different.

So if you start doubting how or what you are writing, by all means ask advice from others (i.e. friends and family) – but know exactly what you are doing. You may well receive helpful feedback, but you need to have a very clear head to 'sort the wheat from the chaff', otherwise you will only end up more confused!

At the end of the day, only *you* know the work and what you are trying to achieve – so trust that. In time, you will anyway. Often it's simply a question of removing yourself from the work for a short time, then coming back to it fresh.

5 Keeping the business

Genuinely care about the work

Conscientious by nature, it comes naturally to me to care about the work – for its own sake *and* to help my client. But I now feel strongly that this attitude is not just good, it is absolutely essential – not only to producing high quality work, but building strong client relationships. It is also the key to deep job satisfaction.

Writing should appear effortless to the reader – it just flows, naturally. In reality, this is the result of many hours of contemplation and refinement (particularly if the subject matter is complex and/or sensitive). You may change your mind many times as you go deeper into the work and obtain greater clarity on structure and messaging.

One who cares about the work therefore keeps going until they are satisfied that it is the best that they can deliver. *The aim is that the client should not have to change anything – or the absolute minimum.*

A clear, fresh mind is obviously important here. I have a rule that I always read through the work once more in the morning before sending over to my client. Reading it afresh always prompts some minor revisions, but even minor revisions can make a big difference to the final outcome.

There is always a point when I know it is finished – you can't tinker forever. There is also a deadline which you must always meet! But the conviction goes deeper than that and you need to trust it.

A client relationship is a partnership

Your contribution to the project may well end with your first draft, if it is accepted in its entirety. But for more complex jobs, it is inevitable that there will be further changes – especially if it is reviewed by several people, not just your immediate contact.

The process of finalising the text is almost always a joint partnership. Even when a client makes minor revisions, I then have to incorporate them to make sure the text/argument still flows etc. The eagled-eyed clarity with which you wrote the initial draft therefore applies equally to any subsequent revisions.

Indeed, you should never be afraid to make suggestions: if you feel strongly about them and are sincerely trying to help, they will always be welcome – and usually incorporated (see Chapter 10, "**Supporting your client**").

Be objective – keep your ego out of it!

Objectivity is really another word for professionalism and goes hand-in-hand with clarity. In other words, you see clearly because your ego is out of the picture. This impacts your work in several important ways:

- If you genuinely desire to do a good job, that will be your focus – not how you will be perceived afterwards. This, in turn, brings clarity and inspiration.

- Personal relationships are part and parcel of the work: keep your ego out of it and you will naturally build good, healthy relationships.

- If there is a genuine cause for grievance, keep anger and emotion out of it. However justified you feel, the blunt truth is that unless the reader feels exactly as you do (which is unlikely), all they will see is anger and emotion – not any valid points you are making. It will also make you look weak and unprofessional.

Emotion obscures clarity

I learnt the dangers of too much emotion myself many years ago when an agency did not pay me, even though they had used my work.

Worried about losing the money and upset that they didn't return my calls, I drafted a stinging letter. However, when I read it to a friend, they said it sounded very emotional (which it probably was!).

So I took all the emotion out – without losing any of the messages – and sent it. The result? The client immediately rang and shamefacedly admitted that they had briefed two copywriters by mistake. A reduced sum was agreed and they even offered me more work. But of course I could never trust them again...

Objectivity does not, of course, apply to the product or service you are writing about. On the contrary, you will be selling it – subtly or overtly – as much as you can! (It goes without saying that you must therefore feel that it is a 'good thing' in principle.)

Stay out of politics

Objectivity is helped by the fact that, as a freelancer, you are beyond the politics of the workplace and therefore free to focus on the work. But don't be complacent: even if you are not interested in politics yourself, you may still find yourself in the middle of it! Indeed, as a neutral figure, you may well find that people confide in you.

This in itself is not a problem; on the contrary, as a sympathetic ear, you may be able to help simply by listening and understanding their point of view. But never get involved yourself: not only do you risk making enemies unnecessarily, it will also distract you from the work which, in turn, will compromise your clarity and efficiency.

The same applies if someone takes exception to you, for whatever reason. If your work is good, there is nothing to fear – unless it takes your focus *away* from the work which will then affect its ultimate quality. No one has the power to stop you doing your best – and that's all you need to be concerned with.

This is not superficial advice. Your attitude and the focus of your attention will create ripples on both an outward *and* subtle level (I wish more people realised this!).

The general rule is therefore: stay out of politics, focus on the work, be efficient – and trust that all will be well.

That's not to say that you should never be assertive; sometimes this is necessary. But it should come from a place of objectivity and clarity, not fear and defensiveness – and always with the best interests of the work at heart.

Cultivate the quality of patience

Patience is a very underrated quality and not appreciated by those who want instant answers – either from the subject matter they are grappling with or their clients vis-à-vis work:

- As far as writing is concerned, experience teaches you to stay focused, dive deep, be patient – and inspiration will surely come.

- As far as work is concerned, you may be impatient to know whether you have won a job and when it will start. But it is always best to give the client space – they will contact you when they are ready. (Of course sometimes you really do need to know, e.g. if projects threaten to overlap, but that is a different matter.)

Being 'desperate' is not only unprofessional, it is also completely unnecessary, as everything resolves itself in time – and usually for the better without your interference.

The general rule is therefore: listen to the inner voice that doesn't need and which is never desperate. That will guide you as to when and when not to act. If you are not familiar with this inner voice – learn to meditate!

Sometimes you just have to wait...

Having already written a couple of reports for an organisation, a conference call then revealed that a letter needed to be written for a high-level audience. Now, all the people on the call were senior executives and quite capable of drafting such a letter themselves. But I was the only professional writer...

Being extremely keen to continue working for them, all I wanted to do was contact the person in charge and volunteer my services. But although this wouldn't have been out of place, I felt that it would be forcing the issue and that it would be much better if the suggestion came from them.

So I forced myself to wait...and wait...and sure enough, a few hours later I received an email asking whether I would write it! My patience was rewarded and I wrote almost every communication after that.

Over time, I have learnt to become very subtle, so that it becomes clear when I should be patient and when/if it is the right moment to speak up. When you don't come from a feeling of desperation, the difference is clear.

Give your client solutions – not problems

The general rule is: take the initiative, wherever possible. You are there to help your client – not give them more problems to solve. This includes every aspect of the work – from messaging to structure to content. If your ideas are sound, your clients will always welcome them.

It is evitable that questions will arise for some projects as you get to grips with the subject matter or messaging. But don't contact them about every little query as it arises – save them up for one conversation. As you go deeper into the work, your queries may also change, while others will resolve themselves naturally.

The very nature of taking the initiative means that you don't constantly ask permission. You do need to cover yourself, however, which means keeping your client informed; and if you are really not sure whether you are over-reaching yourself – ask first.

Design begins with your very first draft

You may think that the only time design comes into play is when your final draft goes off to the studio to be worked up.

Wrong. That's because there are two target audiences here: your client and the ultimate reader. If the client doesn't like the work, there won't *be* an ultimate reader! So first things first. If you present your text in a clear and attractive way – with no mistakes – it will be viewed in the best light possible. It also demonstrates, even before your client has read it, that you are professional and trustworthy.

Of course, the way in which you present the work will heavily influence the design, so you are obviously looking from that angle, too. Indeed, if you are working with a graphic designer, the two are inexorably entwined. However, that tends to be for more agency-driven jobs and campaigns.

For other projects, such as reports, you may well end up managing the design as well as the text, providing a complete service to your client (see page 90).

PART II: THE WORK

6　The art of persuasive writing

Make the best case possible

Persuasive writing is a joy – for the writer *and* the reader, whether they agree with the sentiments or not. Why? Because there is a dynamic quality to it that keeps your attention, carries you along and can make even the dullest of topics seem exciting.

As one point follows another, every sentence seems imperative, the arguments clear and indisputable. Your goal? To make the best possible case for the key issues at stake.

This doesn't mean going over-the-top and writing like a tabloid newspaper – it is far more subtle than that. You can write persuasively and not lose one ounce of credibility or professionalism. Nor is there ever any need, or justification, to distort the facts.

Obviously, everything depends on the objective: there are degrees of writing persuasively and sometimes it isn't even appropriate – for example, when your client wishes to appear neutral.

One thing is very clear, however: there is never any excuse not to present the information in an interesting and readable way!

It goes without saying that you should believe in what you are writing – or at least that it is harmless. I once turned down a commission to write about a product that is proven to cause harm, even though the client insisted that it was simply about brand switching. I never regretted it and it never had any impact on my finances. (Advertising for this product has now been banned.)

Create a good hook

The first sentence, the first paragraph, the first page – indeed the first chapter if it is a report – are absolutely crucial. They set the bar and may well determine whether the reader actually continues reading or not. In this respect it is no different from any book.

In this case, however, you have two readers: the target audience *and* your client! Both must be impressed from the very start. It is not that you should start your piece with some over-the-top statement, but it must be dynamic and persuasive.

Let it read effortlessly

Your work should read effortlessly, without the reader understanding or even questioning why. All they know is that it flows beautifully and is a pleasure to read. This will put them in a good mood to absorb the messages – even feel sympathetic towards them. The joy of the writer then becomes that of the reader in this two-way communication.

The reader is therefore totally unaware of the effort you have taken to work the whole thing out, lovingly fine-tune it and achieve a clear, pristine result. On the downside, the more effortlessly it reads, the easier your client may think it is to write. But you will just have to live with this!

Stay succinct

Succinctness is closely allied with brevity, but it is much more than that, because it is not always possible to keep sentences brief (though you can always avoid repetition).

It is important because it is the key to clarity. If you imagine the opposite of succinctness – verbose, long-winded sentences – you can see how the actual messages would get lost. People are also busy, with limited time and attention span, so will switch off rapidly if reading gets tedious!

Succinctness is pleasing to the ear because points are made clearly, with a minimum of verbiage.

Make every sentence count

A humble writer knows that they never have a captive audience –
it is completely in the power of the reader as to whether they
continue or not. Even if you are giving a speech, the attention of
your audience could be somewhere else altogether. So there is
never any excuse to bore on!

On the contrary, you must come from the premise that no one is
interested in what you write, so you have to make it easy and
enjoyable for them.

Every word and sentence must be there for a reason. If it serves
no purpose – take it out! This means reading your work clearly
and objectively, as your own harshest critic (in the nicest possible
way).

Discrimination is vital

It is vital to discriminate between key messages (and key facts
supporting those messages) and unnecessary information or detail: *this
keeps the messages clear.*

If further explanatory detail is needed, you can either:

a)   Include it in an Annex (if a report)

b)   Use footnotes – not just to provide references, but to free up
     your text and keep it flowing (use sparingly otherwise you will
     achieve the opposite effect!).

Simply put yourself in the shoes of the reader and ask: "Will they be
more convinced knowing this fact, or will it simply 'muddy the
waters'?" The rule is therefore: never include information simply
because you know it, even (or especially) if you are an expert on the
subject. Always discriminate!

There is a corollary to this: sometimes you don't have the luxury of
discriminating due to lack of information. Occasionally, I have had to
make the very most out of the little that was available in order to write
a decent piece. However, it is always possible to disguise the thinness
of the material by writing in an interesting and dynamic way.

Are you creating the right impression?

Impression is everything: it's no good producing beautifully written text, containing all the right messages, if it ends up giving the wrong impression! For example:

- If a new technology is well advanced and virtually ready for market, you would not devote pages of text to any remaining (minor) technical challenges that would then give the opposite impression (unless it is specifically called for, e.g. in response to a tender for funding, to encourage scientific research etc.). At a high level, it is the principle that matters and the key benefits to be gained by society as a result.

- If you are trying to reassure that a product is safe, you may feel that the more you say about it, the more people will be convinced. But instead the reader will think: "Why is there so much emphasis on safety? Is there any *doubt* that it is safe?" Of course, you can't dismiss it if it is an issue that needs to be addressed, but if it's not a major concern, you need to have the subtlety to know when you have said enough to convince – and no more.

- The way to win over your audience is not to criticise the competition: they will simply see fear and weakness. They will know, consciously or unconsciously, that a strong person/ company has no need to put anyone down.

- Finally, it is possible to overstate your case and appear high-handed or desperate – you can't bludgeon a reader into submission! If there are blatant holes in your argument, be in no doubt: the reader will see them. So don't underestimate people's intelligence – you will simply irritate and turn them off. For your argument to work it needs to be sound enough to be held up to scrutiny by even your harshest critic.

To assess whether you are giving the right impression, you simply need to see the words through the eyes of your audience – with humility and objectivity. They may be coming to the subject completely cold; they may feel ambivalent, cynical – even hostile. They could also be very busy or plain bored.

In short, never assume that the reader is on the 'same page' as you. If they were, impression would not matter, as whatever you said would be greeted with approval and enthusiasm!

7   Key principles

Let clarity be your guide

In commercial writing, clarity is king. Your aim is therefore to communicate in such a way that the text flows and is a pleasure to read, the key messages clear and effortlessly absorbed.

Bear in mind that while the facts may be very familiar to you – or they will be once you have written about them! – they may be completely new to the reader. That doesn't mean that you need to 'dumb down'. Just be clear!

Clarity is the result of many things, including:

- Clear messaging (that is supported but not drowned out by detail)

- A clear structure (so information is easy to find and digest)

- A style that is flowing yet succinct (reflecting the joy and objectivity of the writer, i.e. without ego)

- Clear presentation (so text is easy and enjoyable to read)

- Language that is familiar to the reader (if there is any doubt, either don't use it or supply explanations and/or a Glossary). Terminology should also be consistent.

Establish the key messages

Before you start any communications piece, you first need to have clarity on the following:

1. *Who is the target audience?*
   There may well be more than one, so what is the order of priority and who is the most important in achieving your client's goal?

2. *What is the overall objective?*
   What does your client want to achieve as a result of this piece?

3. *What is the key overall message?*
   If there is one message you want the reader to take away, what is it?

4. *What are the secondary key messages?*
   Following on from that, what other messages are important?

5. *What does your client want to happen next?*
   The piece is seldom an end in itself – what specific actions/next steps are required to achieve your client's goal?

These messages are your guiding force – if they do not leap out of the material, you have failed in your job. They should therefore a) shape the structure and b) feature directly in the headings/sub-headings.

Don't wait to be spoon-fed

The more information your client can give you, the better. It doesn't mean you will include every detail – far from it. But the more you understand your subject, the clearer the key messages will be and the more fluently you will be able to write about them.

Naturally, you will quiz your contact as far as you can. But if sufficient guidance is not available, use your own judgement and work it out for yourself. In reality, it will probably be a mixture of the two.

Either way, it's your responsibility to 'sort the wheat from the chaff' and make sure you have got it straight!

Create a clear structure

Your structure is the 'bones' of the piece, so *if a reader does nothing but skim the document, they should be able to absorb the key messages simply by reading the headings/sub-headings*. Indeed, a quick scan of the Contents page should tell them everything they need to know. (It is also a good way to test the logic of your storyline.)

Headings are therefore extremely important because they encapsulate key messages, which may then be reproduced across multiple materials (e.g. presentations, press releases) – as well as in the media. It goes without saying that they should be as punchy and succinct as possible.

With clarity your goal, information should therefore be structured such that:

a)   There is a logical flow to the argument/storyline.

b)   The text is divided up so it is easy to digest.

c)   The various chapters/sections communicate the key messages.

d)   You have discriminated between key messages and extraneous detail. The rule is: include details that support and reinforce the messages – and no more! Other detail can still be included, if necessary, but where it will not drown out the key messages, (e.g. an Annex if a report or a succinct footnote).

e)   The reader can quickly find the information they need without having to trawl through the whole document.

f)   In a report, the Executive Summary should be *a complete story in its own right,* containing all the key messages/information. This is extremely important as it is often the only chapter people will read. If appropriate, you can also insert a Key Conclusions/ Key Recommendations page upfront.

In terms of order, it is best to write the Executive Summary once you have written the rest of the report, when you are totally familiar with the subject matter. You can then write the Key Conclusions/Key Recommendations as a very pithy summary of this. (In terms of priority, however, they come first – see page 50.)

As mentioned earlier, you may well change your mind about the structure as you go deeper into the work and everything becomes clearer. This is completely normal, even inevitable.

Let the text breathe!

The text (and the reader!) needs to be able to breathe. Information is far more attractive to view, and easier to digest, when it is broken down. Imagine a page of text with no paragraphs whatsoever – just the thought of it is enough to make your heart sink!

There are several ways you can achieve this:

- Have a clear structure (see above).

- Use bullets to highlight key messages or avoid long sentences containing a list of details. (In an Executive Summary, the entire text could even be divided into key points as bullets, comprising headline + explanatory text.)

- Use text boxes to highlight key messages, give examples, or simply insert information that doesn't quite fit with the surrounding text (but needs to be included).

- Make sure paragraphs/sections/chapters are not overlong.

- Insert images/graphs etc. at regular intervals (but only if relevant and not so many that they overwhelm the text – clarity also means balance).

- Put text in *italics* and/or **bold** to highlight key messages or differentiate from other text (but sparingly, otherwise you will achieve the opposite effect!).

- Insert key messages as quotations, e.g. as sub-headings or at the beginning of sections/chapters etc. These can come directly from the text itself or from high-level executives within the company and/or respected stakeholders. If you are creating new quotes, you should also be the one to obtain approval, as people sometimes like to tweak their quote and some negotiation may be necessary to keep it on track!

Prioritise, prioritise, prioritise

I don't think I have ever had a deadline that wasn't tight – you are invariably up against it, time-wise. A client will seldom book you in two months in advance; and if they do, they may still not know the exact timing. Then when you get the job, you still have a tight deadline to meet! It's nobody's fault – it's just how business is.

But it does teach you to discriminate and be efficient; and being efficient doesn't just mean being well organised and having a clear mind – it means constantly prioritising. For example, if you are short of time:

- Don't just absorb information quickly, be ruthless about which information is worth studying in detail and which only merits a glance, in your hunt to extract the key messages.

- If you are writing a report, perfect the Executive Summary/Key Conclusions/Key Recommendations first before agonising over less important information elsewhere.

- If you are writing a speech, perfect the beginning and the end over the middle.

- Don't agonise over words and sentences (except the first few paragraphs, if necessary). When you focus on looking clearly and objectively, you can quickly see what works and what doesn't.

Be realistic about time

If it is a large and complicated job, the more time you have the better, as it gives you the chance to contemplate it deeply and do the work justice. But given that you will probably have a range of clients, all acting independently, there will often be occasions when you could do with more time – for the sake of the work *and* your health! Even one extra day can make all the difference.

So never be afraid to ask if it is possible. You have nothing to lose, as long as you make it clear that there is no problem if not (if that is indeed true!).

You must also be realistic, as it is better to turn down a job than do it badly simply because you don't have enough time. To give an extreme example: I was once asked to write a long report, about a subject I knew nothing about, in two days precisely.

I automatically said yes (out of habit), but quickly realised that it was physically impossible! However, as I knew the client didn't want to go to their meeting empty-handed, I came up with a solution that worked for us all: I created a structure instead, as a first step, for approval. I then subsequently wrote the report in a very tight, but more realistic timeframe.

What does editing actually mean?

As well as writing communications from scratch, you may also be asked to edit someone else's rough or even final draft, where the author(s) is an expert on a complex subject, but not a professional writer/communicator. It is actually a very cost-efficient way of using a freelance writer as they don't need to spend time contemplating the content (unless they are very experienced in the subject which is a different matter).

However, you need to be very clear what is possible/required of you: editing is a very broad term for a process that can range from simply correcting the English/grammar to undertaking a total rewrite – including structure, messaging, as well as the text itself. In short, a complete transformation, *yet the content is basically unchanged.*

The answer may depend on several things: time, budget and who has drafted it. For example, if it is a collective effort, you need to be aware of any sensitive issues that have already been hotly debated and resolved before you wade in and start changing things!

Your client may also not be aware of what is actually possible, so it's a good idea to outline your approach first, once you have cast your eye over the text. If you intend to make a lot of changes, the result won't then come as a surprise.

If you know the client well and have undertaken this kind of exercise before, then there will already be a mutual understanding. Even here, however, it is wise to adhere to the following principles:

- Always 'track changes' to show what you have done. The only reason *not* to track changes – or rather save them all before sending on to your client – is when the text is so altered that viewing them becomes a nonsense. This is particularly true of short pieces. For longer pieces (e.g. reports), it is usually best to show all the changes to demonstrate the extent of the work (if necessary, you can make light of it in your covering email and suggest that it will be easier to read with 'track changes' switched off!).

- In some cases (e.g. when sending to a group), it's a good idea to submit two versions (one showing track changes + a clean version with changes saved). Of course it's perfectly possible to view the revised text with this facility switched off, but don't assume everyone knows how to do this – some don't! It therefore doesn't hurt to err on the side of caution, especially for big jobs.

- If you have made a lot of changes, this can result in a sea of colour which could potentially alarm your client. It is therefore crucial to explain your rationale in the covering email (see below) and reassure your client that, despite the number of changes, the content remains unchanged.

- However, if you also change some of the content, you must either be very confident/knowledgeable about the subject, or pass it by your client first to avoid any misunderstanding. Either way, you should highlight and explain content changes by adding 'comments' directly to the text.

Clarity therefore also applies to the way in which you *present* your changes. Always view them through the eyes of your client and never assume something is obvious just because it is to you. After many hours/days of work on a job you will know your revisions inside out, but don't forget that your client is coming to them cold!

Explain your rationale

Whatever the job, I always use a covering email to highlight any aspects of my work I feel would benefit from explanation. With simple jobs this may not be necessary (bar a couple of points). But if you are writing something long, complex or sensitive – especially without an official brief – it is essential to explain your rationale. It may even be necessary to 'sell' or justify your approach.

Either way, it's the email-equivalent of a short presentation before your client reads your work. As always, it should be clear and succinct – a long, tortuous email won't do you any favours (see below)!

Leave no room for doubt

It wasn't until I started writing reports for a stakeholder forum that I realised just how important it was to explain my rationale. In my naivety, I thought that it would be obvious why I had written what I had written and no further explanation was required.

I soon realised that not only was I doing myself a disservice, but that it was easier and clearer for everyone if I explained precisely what I had done and why. Given the sensitivity of the subject, and the range of business interests, it acted as both an explanation and a reassurance (especially if they didn't have time to read the whole draft!).

Apply the same principles to emails

Many fire off emails as if they were of no consequence; and it's true that a quick and efficient response is often all that's required. Most people don't have time to agonise over an email! But you are a freelance writer and have a responsibility to communicate as clearly and helpfully as you can. An email is also a showcase for your writing skills, so there must be no errors or spelling mistakes. Your client can afford to do that – but not you.

An email should therefore be treated like any other communication: it should be clear, succinct and easy to digest. If it isn't, people will just skim over it or even stop reading altogether. It's not unprofessional, it's human nature! Remember: your clients will be extremely busy and bombarded by emails left, right and centre.

So you have to make it easy it for them:

- Never write a long, unbroken block of text. If there's a lot to say, no problem – sometimes this is unavoidable, especially for large pieces of work (your email may include outstanding queries/ requests, as well as explanation).

- The solution is simple: after a short introduction (could be only one or two lines), divide your points into bullets (and sections, if necessary).

- The nature of emails means that you can write in an abbreviated fashion, making the bullets even more succinct.

- Treat the email like any other work, i.e. perfect and edit, as necessary. I can usually reduce my original draft quite considerably – without losing any of the messaging.

Use exclamation marks wisely!

Exclamation marks are an interesting phenomenon: they can be added at the drop of a hat, but not always with the consequences intended...

They seldom find their way into a serious report – they are simply too frivolous and inappropriate. But in other communications, they can convey a lightness and enthusiasm that is attractive (as long as you don't overdo it). The secret is to be acutely aware of the impression created as a result.

Sometimes people use exclamation marks in emails out of fear of appearing cold and unfriendly. This is natural when you are still finding your feet and infinitely better than being pompous! However, you will notice that senior executives do not suffer from that problem, so take your cue from them. There are many ways to convey warmth without losing your dignity.

The answer, as always, is to be sincere. If an exclamation mark feels natural, appropriate and friendly – use it!

8 A style for every occasion

Enjoy the plethora of subjects available

When you truly love writing, you are happy to write about almost any subject – the joy is in the writing, not the content. Nevertheless, it is fascinating to write about a wide range of industries, as you are always learning something new. Each demands a tailored approach – depending on the objective, target audience and medium – and you adapt your style accordingly. One size most definitely does not fit all!

However, I have to be honest and say that as time has gone on, I have developed preferences. For example, it is always motivating to write about something that you feel is important and believe in – this adds another dimension, fuelling your dedication to the work.

It is also very rewarding to write about the same subject over a long period of time. You develop an in-depth understanding that enables you to take even more initiative and provide even more input – taking even more pressure off your client. In fact, you can get to the point where you are basically writing your own brief and managing all the work, which is very satisfying.

There's a time for everything

In recent years, I have focused mainly on sustainable technologies which I have found fascinating, as well as inspiring. The very nature of the subject means that you are at the cutting edge of technology and policy, which is always changing and evolving.

Given that the situation regarding climate change is always critical and the need for action always urgent, it also offers unprecedented opportunities to argue a strong case!

Looking back, however, I can see that there is a time for everything: while there are some subjects that I'm not interested in writing about any more, I certainly didn't feel like that at the time – quite the contrary in fact. But just because you enjoy something at the time doesn't mean you have to repeat the experience endlessly; the simple fact that you have *had* the experience is sometimes enough.

Never lose sight of the ultimate objective

A freelance writer must therefore be able to adapt to *any* industry or medium: one day you could be waxing lyrical over a travel destination (which you have probably never been to!), the next arguing a hard-hitting case for the latest, state-of-the-art technology. Whatever the subject, you know exactly what impression you want to create – and why.

After all, this isn't 'free' writing in the strict sense: even if you work out all the messages yourself, you are not embarking on some ego trip; nor are you writing a novel. *You are writing for your client and therefore never lose sight of the ultimate objective.*

You may also have no control over the final cut: your work could be published verbatim, or go through a long process of approval and revision, depending on your client(s). You may never even see it again until it is finally published!

Where you do have absolute freedom, however, is in the way in which you write and weave all the messages together. The goal? To create a compelling story that's both substantial *and* light at the same time...

Adapt your style according to need

There are literally hundreds of examples of work I could reproduce here, but it's not easy to find ones that 1) don't breach client confidentiality and 2) are not out of date and therefore no longer appropriate for publication (which happens extremely quickly!).

The result is that the examples below are not very complex, despite many years' writing about policy issues at a high level. Nevertheless, they do illustrate that as far as writing styles is concerned, the world is your oyster...

a) Arguing a strong case

You don't have much time to argue a case: even if you have a captive audience, you can still lose their attention very easily, while you have no control whatsoever over a reader. You therefore need to communicate your key messages as clearly and succinctly as possible.

For example,[1] below is a summary of the key benefits of CO_2 Capture and Storage (CCS) technology written for a report[2] published by the European Zero Emission Technology and Innovation Platform (ZEP) – a unique coalition of European oil and gas companies, equipment suppliers, scientists, academics and environmental NGOs, united in their support for CCS in Europe.

These words are even more important as, beyond a brief description of ZEP, they are the very first people will read:

CCS in Europe: critical for jobs, industry *and* the environment

The European Commission has confirmed that Europe cannot be decarbonised cost-effectively – and maintain security of energy supply – without CO_2 Capture and Storage (CCS). Indeed, with fossil fuels currently meeting over 80% of global energy demand and as much as 85 GW of additional capacity expected in Europe alone, CCS is "vital for meeting the Union's greenhouse gas reduction targets".*

Yet the benefits of CCS go far beyond that of climate change mitigation: with annual investments worth billions of euros, CCS will create and preserve jobs, boost industry and fuel economic growth, ensuring Europe remains competitive on the world stage as a leader in low-carbon technologies.

* The European Commission's Communication on CCS, 2013

---

[1] See also examples of speechwriting in Chapter 9
[2] www.zeroemissionsplatform.eu/library/publication/240-me2.html

This illustrates several interesting points:

- The summary is brief as it is not the role of this particular report to go into detail about the benefits of CCS – it would cloud the issue and make the report overlong (and there are other materials for this purpose). However, it is still important to remind the reader upfront of precisely what is at stake.

- When it comes to high-level policy, basing your case on a 'personal view' – even if it is shared by many – is seldom enough; it also needs to be corroborated by an independent source (here, the European Commission).[3]

- When your case consists of several arguments that are all important but distinct (e.g. jobs, climate change), they need to link together effortlessly to create a coherent storyline.

- If a situation demands immediate action, the style and choice of words must reflect that sense of urgency, e.g.:

  🖉 "Critical" is more imperative than "important".

  🖉 "As much as 85 GW" emphasises what is, in energy terms, a very large figure (not all readers may appreciate this).

  🖉 "Indeed" and "Yet" create emphasis, while injecting the text with passion and movement.

  Small details, but it is details such as these that ensure there is no *doubt* as to the significance of the communication.

- When writing about technology, it is often necessary to include terms and phrases that are not succinct but which cannot be shortened. There is therefore even more reason to write in a dynamic way in order to maintain the flow.

- The headline then sums up all the messages in one, succinct phrase.

---

[3] Quotations and statistics should always be backed up with references, but keep footnotes as brief as possible so as not to swamp the communication

b) *Keeping the benefits clear and simple*

The next example comes from a series of magazine advertisements I wrote for a lease-based technology company. The objective? To communicate to Finance Directors that leasing is the most cost-efficient way to manage technology assets:

What's the key to good asset management?

Esc	tax penalties
Ctrl	your cash flow
End	the misery of obsolescence
Shift	to a new way of thinking
Pause	for thought?

You can't operate a business without technology.

But it doesn't have to tie up precious capital. And you don't have to worry about investing in new equipment every time something needs upgrading or packs up.

Why? Because an operating lease from [*company*] not only frees your capital and ends the misery of obsolescence, it reduces your TCO significantly.

How? As an extremely tax-efficient form of finance that combines residual value investment with integrated services, such as insurance and disposal.

The result? A total, flexible solution for the management of *all* your technology assets.

A key factor to bear in mind.

- There is no magic formula here: you simply need to see through the eyes of the reader and accept that they may have no special interest in reading the ad. You have to make it easy for them!

- Key messages are therefore presented as clearly and simply as possible – *with no extraneous detail.*

- The rhetorical, persuasive style ensures that the pace does not let up, hopefully keeping the reader's attention gripped until the end. (The ad obviously contained contact details for easy follow-up.)

c) *Evoking a spirit of wonder*

Arguing a case isn't always the right approach: below is an excerpt from a leaflet I wrote to promote an area of Spain known as Mediterrania. The objective? To counter the impression that it is remarkable only for seaside resorts, such as Alicante and Benidorm, when there is so much more to discover inland:

Mediterrania: the land of contrasts

When the Minstrel in El Cid described the Land of Valencia as "this rich, beautiful, flat land" he was only halfway to the truth. He might also have recounted the wild mountain ridges, deep rugged canyons and dense pine forests, the land of Valencia that is still unknown to many.

So what impression may be captured by visitors to this beautiful region we know as Mediterrania? It could be the ghostly silhouettes of castles, towers and ancient ramparts that etch the skyline, lasting reminders of so many conquering peoples – Carthaginians, Romans, Greeks and Moors.

Or it could be the rich, fertile valleys of orange and lemon groves, rice fields and vineyards, olive trees, fig trees – a cornucopia of flowers and shrubs! How aptly was La Valldigna valley named "valley worthy of a king", its peaceful beauty enhanced only by the 4th century monastery of the same name.

And what of the glorious coastline that is Mediterrania...Costa del Azahar, Valencia and Costa Blanca? It is like one continuous beach, but with an ever-changing character...now long and straight, now secluded in coves; here fine golden sand, there clothed in tiny pebbles. Whether sheltered by jagged cliffs or open to the blue horizon, the beaches of Mediterrania are truly an unforgettable sight.

- This doesn't 'sell' in the traditional sense – that would be too unsubtle and counterproductive. Instead the style is wistful and flowing, evoking an impression of mystery and wonder at the ancient, ever-changing landscape.

- The historical references anchor the region in a time that long precedes the popular seaside resorts of today. Even the coastline is cast in a new light, far removed from the usual hustle and bustle, yet full of life and character.

- It begs the question: do you write better for knowing a place? The answer is yes and no. Yes, because when you know something well, ideas and words inevitably come more easily – you don't need to master the content first. However, I have also written about places I have never visited and while this can take more effort, in the end it makes no difference. I once wrote a brochure on Australia years before I actually went there – and took it with me for reference!

d) Making technology accessible

Turning to CCS technology again, below are excerpts from a brochure[4] describing a key element of the CCS chain: CO_2 storage. Being a relatively new technology, many people don't realise how it actually works, beyond the fact that CO_2 is somehow 'stored' in the ground:

CO_2 has been 'stored' underground for millions of years

The reason why CO_2 storage works is simple: it uses the *same natural trapping mechanisms which have already kept huge volumes of oil, gas and CO_2 underground for millions of years.*

Nor is the technology new: it is almost identical to that used by the oil and gas industry for decades – to increase oil production by injecting CO_2 to 'push' oil towards producing wells, or store natural gas deep underground. Indeed, there are already hundreds of natural gas storage sites worldwide, many found in the most densely populated areas in Europe.

The Intergovernmental Panel on Climate Change (IPCC) therefore confirms it "very likely that the fraction of CO_2 retained will be more than 99% over the first 100 years and likely...(to) be more than 99% over the first 1,000 years". *

* IPCC Special Report on Carbon Dioxide Capture and Storage, 2005

- Any explanation – especially when it is technical – needs to be clear and succinct. These are not academic papers: the target audience invariably ranges from policymakers to the media to the general public. You therefore need to focus on the key facts and make them as simple and accessible as possible.

- You also need to prioritise your messages – not least because there is no guarantee the reader will make it to the end! The very

---

[4] www.zeroemissionsplatform.eu/library/publication/17-what-is-co-2-storage.html

first paragraph of the brochure therefore highlights the most important feature of CO_2 storage: that it is not actually new at all – either in nature or industry. Confidence in its efficacy is then backed up again by an independent source (here, the IPCC).

- The text follows a tight, logical – but rhetorical – sequence: no words are redundant. Starting sentences with linking words such as "Nor" and "Indeed" keep up the momentum (but must not be overused), while the third paragraph brings the matter to a decisive conclusion.

CO_2 storage becomes even more secure over time

This is how it works: the CO_2 is compressed into a dense fluid then pumped – via one or more wells – into a porous geological formation, around a kilometre underground. At first, being more buoyant than water, it rises to the top of the formation, where it becomes trapped beneath a layer of impermeable cap-rock which acts as a seal – the same cap-rock that has trapped oil, gas and CO_2 underground for millions of years.

However, it is not long before other trapping mechanisms also start to take effect: during injection, and as the CO_2 shifts within the formation, it becomes trapped in the tiny pore spaces of the rocks and does not move. The CO_2 also starts dissolving into the water and being heavier than the water around it, sinks to the bottom of the formation, trapping it indefinitely. Finally, the dissolved CO_2 reacts chemically with the rocks to produce minerals.

- The second excerpt then describes the process behind CO_2 storage as simply as possible – with no frills.

- Finally, headings in both excerpts reduce and encapsulate the key messages.

e) Creating a positive impression

I wrote several hundred recruitment advertisements for a large NHS hospital trust, spanning the whole gamut of positions and departments – from phlebotomists to radiographers to senior sisters. I was supplied with a detailed job description from which I then had to extract the key elements and create the ad. For example:

PART-TIME

PHARMACY ASSISTANT

[*Salary*]

You *know* you can do it! And it's great fun, too. As a Pharmacy Assistant, you'll be working with a huge variety of people as you manage and dispense pharmaceutical supplies to the wards and departments of [*London*] Hospitals NHS Trust. In fact, it's the perfect prescription for anyone who's returning to work or looking for something a bit different.

Dispense with modesty.

You'll get involved in all the nitty gritty of distribution – from receiving and putting together pharmaceutical orders, to providing a 'top-up' service to wards and departments. You'll also be responsible for compiling requisitions and making regular stock and expiry date checks.

It means being organised and reliable, having good spoken and written English, and basic numeracy. And it's only for 20 hours a week – 08.30am-12.30pm, Monday to Friday.

So if you can dispense with modesty to take on a truly satisfying job, talk to [*name*] on [*telephone number*] to find out more today.

- As the jobs themselves did not differ greatly from equivalent positions in other hospitals, it was essential to come from another angle: in this case, by presenting the information in a humorous and upbeat way, led by an eye-catching headline. This not only attracts the attention of the reader, it gives a very positive impression of the job itself.

- This particular position was not highly paid and did not demand previous experience, so it was even more important to encourage people who may otherwise have dismissed the idea.

- I had to be ruthless (and quick) about choosing which elements of the job to focus on: the job description ran to several pages and the ad had limited space.

- It obviously did the trick as my client told me that responses went from a trickle to over 200 for one position! It was an enjoyable exercise and with a several coming in every month, represented 'bread and butter' work that was much appreciated at the time.

f) Inspiring enthusiasm

I have written several in-house magazines for employees/dealers/wholesalers over the years, the idea being to foster loyalty towards the company in question. This task should not be underestimated: just because such a magazine exists, it doesn't mean the target audience will read it!

For example, below is an excerpt from a bimonthly magazine produced for dealers of a well-known car manufacturer. Along with several other writers, I was given the theme for various articles, the space available (e.g. half page) and the freedom to write them any way I wished. This included interviewing the dealer/customers directly to get the full story and any quotes:

A world of difference

When [*x car dealer*] took over nearby [*y car dealer*] 18 months ago, they knew they couldn't keep the site as it was. Nearly 60 years old – and showing it – there was only one solution: pull it down and build a new one! And between July and December last year, that's precisely what they did.

The new showroom covers exactly the same area as before, but through creative and efficient design, actually appears much bigger. Indeed, not only has the existing workshop been totally refurbished, a brand new Service Centre has been added as well. There's also a new customer viewing area overlooking the workshop and more parking room outside.

In line with [*the car manufacturer's*] new corporate image, the new look is modern, light and airy, and extremely impressive in terms of presentation. As [*x car dealer's CEO*] put it, *"It looks superb – more like a space terminal than a garage!"*

And the customers certainly seem to agree. Compliments have been flooding in, the general consensus being that it is now a very attractive and comfortable environment in which to do business.

Or as one enthusiastic customer put it, *"Your new building's just amazing!"*

- Obviously, the article was accompanied by photos/illustrations, but that alone will not encourage readership. As always, you have to make it easy for your audience: not by writing in a puerile way, but by making the articles enjoyable and inspiring to read, which in turn reflects positively on the company.

- You basically search for, and amass, a list of interesting points, then find a way of weaving them all together in a natural and readable way.

- If the points aren't that interesting, you can always compensate with a good quote. If this doesn't manifest in the course of your interview, that's okay – you can simply create one yourself and have it approved by the dealer etc. (If you approach this diplomatically, it is highly unlikely they will refuse, unless the subject matter is sensitive/controversial, in which case some negotiation may be required.)

- Once again, it is a case of using your initiative and sorting everything out, thus taking maximum pressure off your client.

g) *Making it fun!*

The final example may not even qualify as business writing, but the aim was certainly to boost business! The brief? To write a series of murder/mystery stories, each printed on the reverse of a drinks mat (for bars, pubs, clubs etc.). The objective? To encourage people to drink a famous cocktail known as a Blue Lagoon.

The drinker was invited to solve the mystery, then place their glass onto a coded panel on the front of the drinks mat, whereupon the blue colour of the cocktail reacted with the panel to reveal the answer:

Mysteries of the Blue Lagoon/No.1

Even the glorious sunset, spreading its colourful cloak over the Indian summer evening, could not dim the brilliance of the Eastern Diamond which, like a magnet, attracted all those who beheld it...

As we enjoyed supper that cool night, it sparkled tantalisingly on the turban of Georgina Ponsonby. "Darlings, isn't it just divine?" she said, "I glued it on myself only this evening."

The night grew colder. The soup became hotter. And everyone forgot to admire the Eastern Diamond and began to admire Georgina instead...

George was besotted. His eyes glowed as, devotedly, he rearranged the headdress that threatened to fall over her eyes. And Peter was quick to deal bravely with a fly that landed on her head as she bent to sip daintily the concoction before her. But it was Charles who, coming up behind her, playfully covered her eyes.

Georgina threw up her hands in delight. "Charles, it must be...Charles! My diamond – it's gone! Who has taken my diamond?"

There was silence. One man looked at another, but I looked deep into my Blue Lagoon.

"I think," I said, "you'll find....................holds the answer.

"How on earth did you know?" she later asked adoringly.

"Naturally," I replied, "I found my inspiration in the Blue Lagoon".

- My only instructions were to:

  1) Create an impression of old-world glamour
  2) Keep the stories to around 200 words
  3) Refer to the cocktail in the final line.

  Otherwise, I had a completely free rein.

- Given the audience, setting and product, the stories obviously had to be fun and light-hearted. The plot also had to be relatively easy to solve, but not so simple it would bore and patronise the audience.

- Creating a story of only 200 words which is not only exciting, but contains enough clues to solve a mystery, is not easy; my own first draft was always much longer than that! However, it was then very satisfying to reduce it further and further, retaining just enough detail to make it playful, while keeping the story tight and succinct.

- The answer, in case you hadn't guessed, was "*your soup*"! The heat of the soup melted the glue on the diamond...

9   Speechwriting: set your rhetoric free!

Make the script sound completely natural

I have attended many conferences and I have to be honest: the best speeches are those that are given without recourse to a script. Why? Because the delivery is automatically natural and flowing (assuming, of course, they are fluent speakers!).

In reality, however, the content is often too complex and sensitive for memory alone (and the last thing you want to do is read loads of small text on a slide verbatim).

The job of the speechwriter is therefore twofold:

1) To determine the key messages and storyline

2) To deliver this in such a way that there is *no difference between your script and the spoken word.* If you have any doubts, simply read it aloud and you will soon hear if anything sounds stiff or jars.

The joy of speechwriting is that you don't have to conform to the usual restrictions of grammar and syntax. You can introduce all kinds of colloquialisms at your leisure. You can emphasise words, create dramatic pauses – whatever you like to make the script sound completely natural (although if it's going to be published afterwards you will need to bear this in mind).

But that doesn't mean it ends up an unstructured 'brain dump'. On the contrary, the rules of discrimination, clarity and succinctness are more important than ever. No one wants to hear someone droning on, without direction or a tight grasp of the messages.

Never assume you have a captive audience

Indeed, to imagine that you have a captive audience is both deceptive and naive. While you are speaking, there is nothing whatsoever to stop people's attention from wandering – to their thoughts, their phone, their neighbour. At the end of your speech, it is quite possible that nothing has gone in at all! This is even more likely if you are unfortunate enough to speak at the end of a conference when everyone is tired and ready to go home.

Instead, the speaker has an unrivalled opportunity to take the audience on a journey that is both inspiring and entertaining – not in the sense that it is a laugh a minute, but in that they are a genuine joy to listen to.

That's because it's not just about the content, important though this is. It's the way it is *presented* – and in the case of speeches, also *delivered* – that makes the difference. It's also why it's possible to make even the dullest subject sound interesting (and vice versa)!

For example, below is the beginning of a 20-minute conference speech I wrote for a multinational organisation about a new low-carbon technology. In the interests of confidentiality, I can't include any information about the organisation itself, but I can demonstrate how a simple point (here, the need to remove market barriers) can be communicated in an interesting and compelling way:

"Mission possible"

It's time to bring Hydrogen to market

Once upon a time – the mid 1980s in fact – there was a revolutionary new technology that promised to change people's lives forever. A technology whose usefulness – both commercially and privately – appeared indisputable. And yet it was nearly 10 years before it finally got off the ground.

How could this be, you may ask? How could a technology so obviously beneficial take so long to become accepted and established? Several reasons:

1) It was capital-intensive and in the beginning, the infrastructure simply wasn't there. 2) It wasn't stable and performance improved only gradually over time. 3) There was very little competition, so pricing was high. And finally, there were potential health concerns about its uptake.

In short, consumers just didn't buy it.

What is this technology? Well, if you haven't already guessed, it's our old friend, the all-pervasive, digital mobile phone. And how attitudes have changed...networks are comprehensive and stable; costs have tumbled; and health concerns have largely subsided.

And the moral of the story? That it doesn't matter how great is the promise of Hydrogen technology...how limitless its potential...how environmentally friendly compared to fossil fuels. Unless the barriers to its market entry are resolved, it will remain just that – a promise.

- My client didn't supply me with this information: I came up with the idea – all they had to do was approve it. It's not that you are required to do this every time – you are not a journalist – but you should always be interested and motivated enough to take the initiative, where appropriate.

- Enthusiasm is key to engaging your audience – not childish or over the top, but a genuine conviction that your product/service/ argument is positive.

- While carefully crafted to be persuasive and succinct, the script still sounds natural and spontaneous.

The second example is an excerpt from a conference speech given by the CEO of an international hotel group. Before I wrote it, I knew nothing about the principles of Asset Ownership, let alone Sale & Leaseback. However, my brief was to explain his clear views on both:

Why Asset Ownership remains the best strategy

Good morning! It's very good to be here and to have the opportunity to talk about a subject that's very close to my heart: the advantages and rewards of Asset Ownership. And the corresponding pitfalls of Sale & Leaseback...

Assets are a funny thing. They offer the potential to create even *more* wealth out of what you already have – clearly, that's the principle behind every successful hotel business. But they're like a delicate treasure. Unless you look after them, you could lose them altogether...

The practice of Sale & Leaseback has been around for a long time – and still hasn't lost its appeal. Indeed, several major hotel companies have taken this route, using the proceeds to fund their expansion.

What's wrong with that, you may ask? You have to speculate to accumulate and [*hotel group*] has succeeded in broadening its portfolio in one fell swoop! And that's the attraction of this arrangement: by selling your assets and leasing them back again, you can unlock shareholder value and use it to greater advantage. Indeed, by reducing the capital invested, you can increase the percentage return. If your strategy is one of expansion, you can even recycle the capital again with a further round of Sale & Leaseback deals.

That's the theory anyway.

But you don't get something for nothing and in this case, the price is the rent. No problem...as long as you can pay it. Because if anything untoward happens – and let's face it, we've had our fair share of such events recently – you could find yourself in breach of your lease payments. This is no far-fetched scenario – it's happened to one very well-known hotel group already.

Because the truth is, you can only sell your assets once and once you have done so, you are locked into a fixed moment in time. You have not only thrown away your security, you have also now incurred a debt. And with interest rates at their lowest for many years, it is far from the cheapest way of borrowing...

- The CEO wasn't addressing an audience of laymen – this was a conference for hotel professionals. This meant that the speech had to contain real 'meat' to be of interest; a superficial account would not suffice. I therefore had to make sure I really understood the arguments first (quickly, as always!) before I could weave them together into a convincing story.

- In order to present a credible argument it's often necessary to fully address the opposing view so that there are no 'ifs or buts' left in the minds of the audience. It also demonstrates that you have a complete understanding of the issues at stake.

- Despite sounding very natural, there is no let up in the flow of argument – no extraneous 'puff'. Remember: never take the attention of your audience for granted!

Start and end on a compelling note

Ideally, the entire speech will be interesting and compelling – but especially at the beginning and end. It needs a strong hook to attract the attention of the audience and a dynamic finish, as *that* is what they will have ringing in their ears as the speaker leaves the podium.

For example, here is the beginning of a conference speech that launches with a provocative statement, this time to an audience of oil and gas professionals:

"The customer rules OK"

A transformation in European downstream marketing

Thank you, [*name*]. Good afternoon! [*This conference*] seems to come around more quickly every year. But I welcome the opportunity for us to share our thoughts and experiences at a time of such rapid change.

It's a well-worn phrase: the customer comes first.

But how many companies actually live this? Certainly, the *traditional* value chain in the oil business began with the resource. We searched for – and found – oil; produced it, refined it, then sold it to the consumer. In short, the retail operation was always at the *end* of the chain – not the beginning.

Not anymore.

Indeed, I would argue that in the downstream sector our value chain is being stood right on its head. It is a shift so fundamental that it amounts, in many respects, to a virtually new business model. Today, for a company to be successful in this highly competitive and fickle industry, its enterprise strategy must start – not end – with the customer.

- There are usually a few introductory words, (e.g. thanking the link man, commenting on the nature of the conference, a humorous aside etc.) before the speaker gets 'stuck in'. But unless you have something appropriate to say, this can be limited to a simple "Good Morning" etc. or even nothing at all – an experienced speaker will be more than capable of supplying these words themselves; it may even sound more natural.

- Rhetorical questions (*"But how many companies actually live this?"*) should not be overused, but are very effective in injecting dynamism.

- It's not always possible to maintain this level of dynamism for the entire script – there are often too many corporate details that have to be included. Nevertheless, you should always maintain the momentum and make the facts sound as interesting as possible.

The end of a speech is basically a conclusion, a rallying cry or a specific call to action – possibly all three. Either way, it should be clear, heartfelt and dramatic.

For example, this is the end of a speech I wrote for an annual meeting of technology leaders. The speaker makes an impassioned case for innovation and the key role played by business in turning it into commercial reality:

"Making it real"

The role of business in science and innovation

Innovation has been described as creativity + implementation. Certainly, without ideas, there can *be* no innovation; but without implementation, ideas remain just that.

The missing link is business: it has the incentive, the capability and the experience to take ideas and turn them into commercial reality.

And it does so, again and again – a true solution provider to the challenges society faces, driven by the desire to meet and *exceed* customer expectations.

Like all links, however, it is just one in a chain. It cannot succeed alone. The key to any lasting progress therefore lies in partnerships – between the public and private sector, government and industry. And the greater the stability government can provide, the more likely business will innovate, delivering the *vital* economic growth society needs to develop and grow.

Because the truth is, we are *all* in this together and we at [*company*] are more than willing to play our part.

Thank you.

- This is a clear call to action and the audience will be in no doubt as to the key message/conclusion of the speech.

- Italicising some words can aid delivery, but don't feel obliged to do this for every sentence – only when it feels natural.

- Ultimately, it is not a question of using this word or that, but of creating a flow that is akin to music to an objective, well-trained ear.

Communicate confidence, not arrogance

Unlike a written piece, the speaker is almost as important as the script. I once watched senior executives deliver speeches I had written with totally contrary results: one spoke so naturally you would never have known he was reading from an autocue; the other sounded so wooden I could hardly bear to watch!

As the writer of the script, you obviously have no control over delivery; but you can certainly control the tone. I have seen a speaker rapidly lose the goodwill of his audience by talking down to them, using long, tortuous sentences, apparently trying to bludgeon them into submission!

Unless you are preaching to the converted, you can't force an audience to your way of thinking through sheer force of will; and people know the instant they are being patronised. In other words, an audience always knows where you are coming from (even if politeness inhibits them from saying so!).

Confidence and conviction, on the other hand, are very attractive, as the speaker then imbues the script with dynamism and authenticity. If you are lucky enough to write a speech for someone with these qualities – but with no trace of arrogance – it will be delivered precisely as intended.

Do you need to meet the speaker?

I have often been asked this question and the assumption is that every speech must be tailored to the personality of the speaker. In an ideal world, perhaps!

In reality, there isn't usually time for such luxuries when you are writing speeches for a range of executives, across different business sectors, often in different countries – all within one organisation! You might get the chance to speak to them on the phone, but that's all.

Personally, I have never felt it was a problem and nor have my clients. After all, if the executive is senior enough to warrant a speech being written for them, they are usually experienced and confident enough to deliver it.

Of course, it's always nice if you do know them well. I wrote many speeches for one client and used to imagine him delivering it, reassured by the fact that he was an excellent speaker who I knew would give full power and justice to the script!

After-dinner speech? Lighten the mood!

Now, after-dinner speeches are a slightly different breed from your average conference speech. Why? Because the mood has changed: the wine's flowing, everyone's relaxed and there's an expectation that you are going to be entertained, not just informed.

That's not to say you can't deliver important messages and that every sentence must contain a joke – it's not a wedding speech! But there must be humour and a lightness of touch. For this reason, it's even more important to read your speech aloud – exactly as it would be delivered – so that you can be sure it will sound natural and relaxed.

As for the jokes/funny stories: it's not easy to find something that fits and you need to be *really* honest about whether it works – better to have no jokes than have one that falls flat on its face. However, my experience is that if you look hard enough – and there are many books written specifically for this purpose – you will eventually find something you can weave in.

As for the serious messages: it's not a question of imparting these with humour, but of employing rhetoric to make them sound dynamic and compelling. Rhetoric, when used skilfully, can be as 'entertaining' as any joke. It's just a question of alternating seamlessly between the two.

For example, here is the beginning of an after-dinner speech I wrote for a GP to other GPs on the thorny topic of migraines:

"It's a real headache!"

A GP's perspective on migraines

Good evening! It probably comes as no surprise to see me here, to discuss an area of our practice in which I am professed an expert. You've seen someone like me – or very like me! – many times before. *This* time, however, there's a difference. Because not only do I *not* profess myself to be an expert in this subject, I plead a positive ignorance. In fact, I would describe my management of migraine patients as anything but first class!

But I'm not here to cast judgement – on myself *or* others. Rather, I want to suggest why incompetence in this area is not only understandable, it's downright forgivable – and *then* to suggest the nature of the advice we need to rectify such woeful ignorance.

But first let us consider the nature of the beast. What do medical textbooks actually tell us about headaches? In general practice, not a lot. I have to admit that I personally find it one of the most difficult problems to solve, as well as one of the least rewarding.

Let's take a typical scenario. It may ring a familiar bell!

It's Friday evening, it's 6.30, and surgery was *supposed* to have finished half an hour ago. But that has no bearing on the fact that you've still got two more patients to see – *and* a visit on the way home. Which is a pity, because tonight also happens to be School Prize Giving which, having missed last year, you faithfully promised to attend. Where is your surgery partner? Oh, he's away attending a mandatory course on Interactive Therapy. Get the picture? I thought you might.

So, in walks your next patient. What are you thinking? You've guessed it..."Please let it be a sore throat".

He sits down. He clears his throat. And he utters those terrible words..."Doctor, I've been having these headaches."

At this point, you may register one of several reactions:

    a) "Oh good!"   b) "Oh no!"   c) "Oh ****!"

You may, of course, register none of these. But why *does* the very mention of headaches strike such foreboding within us? It may be because headaches in general practice are associated with such a low frequency of serious pathology...yet a *high* incidence of non-organic disease.

- While the speech continues thereafter in a more technical vein, the style shows the light touch appropriate to an evening meeting.

- All the rules of grammar have been thrown aside, where necessary. It's not that you should go wild, just that the script needs to be written *exactly* as it will be delivered and after-dinner speeches, in particular, are unlikely to be published.

Declutter presentations

The worst kind of presentation is where as much text as possible is crammed onto the slides, which the speaker then proceeds to read verbatim. You don't get more tedious than that! Certainly, slides are a helpful aide-memoire for the speaker, but they should be far too concise and abbreviated to represent a script.

While a presentation should comprise a complete story in itself (especially if it is to be published), that is no excuse to overload it. On the contrary, it represents the perfect opportunity to communicate an easy-to-absorb summary of all the key messages – and a summary is precisely what it should be!

You will either be required to write a presentation from scratch or edit/improve someone else's draft. I have never received a presentation where it hasn't been possible to reduce/edit the text – without losing *any* of the messaging. It can be a very satisfying exercise! But even if you write the presentation yourself, you will still go through the process of refining and reducing it until you achieve the desired result.

Presentations should therefore be clear, succinct and attractive:

- *Every slide heading should communicate a key message.* Remember that the usual rules of grammar do not apply here: headings and bullets can all be abbreviated to exclude pronouns, articles, verbs etc., if appropriate. The only rule is that it should make sense and be clear to the reader.

- *The text must be able to breathe*: as well as keeping bullets succinct, there should be a liberal amount of white space, where possible. (It goes without saying that text should also be large enough to read easily from afar.)

- Given that an attractive and colourful presentation is much more likely to be read and absorbed, *a sprinkling of images is always helpful* – it brings the text alive. But even text-only slides can be improved through the use of colour, bullets, arrows, text boxes etc. Be creative!

- *Keep the number of slides to a minimum*: too many and you will disrupt the flow of the speech – for the speaker *and* audience. Too much focus on the slides is also tiring for the audience who should be 'entertained', but not exhausted!

Even if you are not required to produce the slides, you should still insert (short) headings in your script at regular intervals to reflect the key messages. This gives structure to the speech and is essential for publication or reading by an internal audience.

10   Supporting your client

Give your best, honest advice

There is an art to incorporating comments/revisions from clients and colleagues. Clearly, if you have one client and they want to change something, your job is to accommodate them as best you can. However, if you are serving several people within one organisation, your task is more complicated – even delicate. Why? Because comments may not only be uncoordinated, they may even contradict!

Some will be good and/or non-negotiable, others you may strongly disagree with. If you are focused on doing the best job possible, the difference will be clear. As a freelancer who is paid to offer their best advice, it is therefore your duty to give it – even if it is at odds with the views of your client.

It's all about delivery. Most people will appreciate the genuine care behind the advice which, if delivered humbly and tactfully, could very well be taken. However, it is essential that it is practical and precise (i.e. actual words/changes) not some vague suggestion that will simply ring alarm bells. Remember: your job is to provide solutions, not problems!

There is always a solution

In stakeholder fora, the stakes are even higher as you may be dealing with many different organisations, nationalities and business interests. While all the above still applies, you therefore need to be even more sensitive and diplomatic. There must be no question of your favouring any particular organisation or business interest.

Instead, *your allegiance is to the work itself, in your understanding of the ultimate objective.* To this end, it may be necessary to resist some comments as too extreme, one-sided or inappropriate. Indeed, it is seldom possible to include *every* suggestion without the document ending up a mess!

You do, however, need to be flexible. While you may have very clear ideas about the best way to communicate something, you can't be precious about it. Sometimes you have no choice but to make changes that you don't like, or ruin the flow of your carefully crafted text! At the end of the day, everyone who puts their name to the document has to be happy with it.

There is one thing, however, that you *always* have control over – and that is giving your best. This is not some soppy, motivational statement, but a profound truth. Such dedication will ensure a constant flow of ideas and Eureka moments in your sincere desire to help. As Editor, you can also ensure that all (necessary) comments are carefully edited and incorporated.

The good news is, whether the issue is a political minefield or a minor word change, there is always a solution. Sometimes it's not immediately obvious, but time and patience reveal it eventually. There is never any need to panic.

Trust comes with experience

After working for a stakeholder forum for many years, the difference between the veterans and the newcomers was very easy to see...

With so many different members and business interests, it was inevitable that there would be differences of opinion along the way. However, where the newcomers sometimes panicked that such differences must be irreconcilable, the veterans didn't bat an eyelid. They had seen it all before!

The veterans knew that somehow, in some way, a solution would come. They didn't even need to know what form this would take straightaway, they just knew that it would be resolved in the end; it always was.

It's the same as when you start on a difficult project trusting that you can do it, even though you don't know, in the beginning, precisely how it will work out. It's basically a leap of faith borne out by experience.

It's a very relaxing way to be!

Diplomacy wins all

Keeping everyone happy simply means a) being genuinely open to all suggestions/revisions and b) giving an appreciative and diplomatic response.

The golden rule is: *there is never any reason for anyone to lose face.* Indeed, this must be avoided at all costs – not only because it is inconsiderate, but because people do not take kindly to appearing foolish in front of their colleagues. Even if you are 100% right – and they can see that you are right – this will be no compensation.

If you are in a position where it is necessary to reject some comments, the following may therefore help:

- Avoid a total rejection, if possible. For example, if you receive seven suggestions from one reviewer and don't agree with any of them, try and include at least one. You should then explain (very tactfully) why it is not possible (or necessary) to include the others.

- You can refute comments in a non-personal way – for example, by responding that unfortunately it is not possible to include their suggestion as you are obliged to go with the views of the majority.

- You can demonstrate why the negative impact they fear (on their business) is not justified, but be realistic as to whether this is actually true, otherwise your resistance will simply irritate.

- Never let the debate become a fight: even if you win, you risk losing the goodwill of the other, which not only threatens the harmony of the group, it could damage your relationship.

If your goodwill is sincere, however, even rejection can be delivered in such a way that the receiver doesn't actually feel rejected at all. On the contrary, they appreciate your honesty and sincerity. It helps if you genuinely like people!

Running a tight ship

Very often the resolution to a difficult or controversial comment is neither acceptance nor rejection, but a compromise reached through delicate and amicable negotiation.

For example, I once wrote a report for a forum where one group was very keen to emphasise a particular policy aspect. Fearing that it would be insufficiently represented, they revised the text so that it was mentioned five times in as many pages. The result: a complete mess! But it was an issue that clearly needed to be addressed.

I was able to satisfy this group (and the rest of the forum) by:

1. Acknowledging their legitimate concerns (*you appreciate the issue at stake*)

2. Including the point upfront in the Executive Summary and once more in the remaining text (*you provide a clear, practical solution*)

3. Highlighting that as long as the point was made clearly, it wasn't necessary to keep making it, thus maintaining the balance and clarity of the document (*you explain why your solution works – for them and everyone else*).

If queries are resolved by telephone – the most diplomatic medium for thorny issues – *always* follow up with an email, confirming in writing what has been agreed and copying in anyone who also needs to be aware of it (but keep the number to a minimum so as not to appear too heavy-handed).

This is important in order to:

a)   Ensure there are no misunderstandings going forward

b) Keep discussions open and transparent (you should always be prepared for your email to be passed on to others)

c) Cover yourself.

Be warm, but always professional

It has to be said: emails can be very misleading. Unless the recipient knows you well, it is very easy for a professionally written email to sound cold. Now 'professional' is, of course, good and you certainly don't want to come across as gushing or overfamiliar. If you are not sure, simply respond in the same manner as your client and you can't go wrong.

But if you wish to come across as professional *and* friendly, there is a middle way...it simply means being aware of how you write and the impression that is created as a result.

It basically means being sincere. My experience is that natural warmth always comes through and there are as many ways to express this as there are people...

Seek to help, not impress

There is a misapprehension that in order to appear capable, one must speak up in a meeting, whether you have anything worthwhile to say or not. This is unwise for two reasons: firstly, if your motivation comes from a desire to impress and a fear of obscurity, then your ideas and words will not come from clarity. Secondly, be in no doubt – people will see right through you! In this case, it would be better just to stay quiet.

If, on the other hand, you genuinely feel that you have something useful to say – not in order to impress but because it feels imperative – then this will shine through your words. Even if you feel fear while you are speaking it doesn't matter – the imperative feeling will take care of that.

If you care about the work, rather than yourself, clarity and ideas will inevitably come. Just sit back and watch yourself speaking!

Communication doesn't stop at words...

Communication isn't just about the written or spoken word – it's often bound up with image, too. It is therefore a natural progression for you to get involved in the design as well as the writing process, should the opportunity arise (i.e. when working directly with the client, as opposed to via an agency). Indeed, you must be ready for this.

Clearly, the graphic designer is the expert here, but even they won't know the subject like you do and the subtleties of the impression you want to create. However good the design concept, there are therefore usually changes that need to be made and you must always be open and honest in this regard. Even minor changes – such as the size and placement of headlines and images – can make a big difference to the overall effect.

In essence, you apply the same objective scrutiny that you do to your own written work and as with your own work, you settle for nothing less. If you want to achieve an effect but don't know how, simply ask the designer for help. It is a two-way process and they understand that their first version is seldom the last. I'm very grateful for everything that designers have taught me over the years!

Why limit yourself?

Although your remit is writing and communications, there will always be a cross-over with other disciplines. In large companies, the strategy will usually be set; but in smaller ones, or areas where there is greater flexibility, there really is no limit to the advice that you can offer (as long as it is good!).

It will only be good if you adhere to the principles described above, which means only offering advice where it feels right and/or appropriate. For example, before I started any new project, one client liked me to come in and spend a couple of hours brainstorming in order to determine where to go next. I found it extremely interesting and would probe with questions in order to help clarify the objective and subsequent strategy.

You can also help your client by taking the pressure off them in other areas by:

- Determining the theme/storyline/key messages of the communication

- Undertaking any additional research

- Liaising with relevant colleagues/stakeholders

- Managing all comments/revisions

- Managing the design and layout

- Managing print

...all the way up to full project management.

After all, anything is possible. So why not set your sights high, do what you really want to do – and fulfil your *true* potential?

About Hermione St. Leger

After reading Modern History at Lady Margaret Hall, Oxford, Hermione St. Leger tried various advertising-related jobs before realising that writing was her true love.

She now has over 20 years' freelance experience in writing and managing all forms of corporate communication, including brochures, conference speeches, reports, presentations, editorials, articles, advertisements etc.

This has encompassed a whole range of sectors – from energy, technology, science and health to finance, travel and automotive. In recent years, however, she has focused increasingly on sustainable technologies, such as CO_2 Capture and Storage (CCS), Hydrogen and Fuel Cells, Biofuels, Wind Energy and Solar.

This includes working for international companies, as well as stakeholder fora such as European Technology Platforms initiated by the European Commission. It also includes full project management, liaising with a broad range of parties in order to maximise impact, reconcile business interests and find solutions that are attractive to all.

Clients have included Royal Dutch Shell, European Zero Emission Technology and Innovation Platform (ZEP), McKinsey & Company, Fuel Cells and Hydrogen Joint Undertaking, European Energy Research Alliance (EERA), SINTEF, North Sea Basin Taskforce, Oil and Gas Climate Initiative, Hewlett-Packard, Barclays Bank, Novotel, Gillette, General Motors and European Commission-funded projects, DYNAMIS and ULTimateCO2.

For more information, please write to:
lovelettertobusinesswriting@gmail.com

www.ingramcontent.com/pod-product-compliance
Lightning Source LLC
Chambersburg PA
CBHW050545280326
41933CB00011B/1723